# Pablo Neruda

# Pablo Neruda

## Passion, Poetry, Politics

## JODIE A. SHULL

**Enslow Publishers, Inc.**
40 Industrial Road
Box 398
Berkeley Heights, NJ 07922
USA

http://www.enslow.com

*For Russell, Poet and Painter*

**Library of Congress Cataloging-in-Publication Data**

Shull, Jodie A.
    Pablo Neruda : passion, poetry, politics / Jodie A. Shull.
       p. cm.
    Summary: "Explores the life of famed Chilean poet Pablo Neruda, including his childhood in Chile, his poetry, and the many political causes he fought for"—Provided by publisher.
    Includes bibliographical references and index.
    ISBN-13: 978-0-7660-2966-8
    ISBN-10: 0-7660-2966-2
    1. Neruda, Pablo, 1904–1973—Juvenile literature. 2. Authors, Chilean—20th century—Biography—Juvenile literature. I. Title.
PQ8097.N4Z788 2008
861'.62—dc22                                                2008008698

Printed in the United States of America

10 9 8 7 6 5 4 3 2 1

**To Our Readers:** We have done our best to make sure all Internet Addresses in this book were active and appropriate when we went to press. However, the author and the publisher have no control over and assume no liability for the material available on those Internet sites or on other Web sites they may link to. Any comments or suggestions can be sent by e-mail to comments@enslow.com or to the address on the back cover.

♻ Enslow Publishers, Inc., is committed to printing our books on recycled paper. The paper in every book contains 10% to 30% post-consumer waste (PCW). The cover board on the outside of each book contains 100% PCW. Our goal is to do our part to help young people and the environment too!

# Contents

## Acknowledgments

With thanks to Edith, Judith, Donna, Karen, Connie, Suzan, Stephanie, Marie, and Nina— teachers and women of wisdom!

# 1

# "He Is Pablo Neruda"

A tall, heavy man in a pinstriped suit hurried into a crowded meeting hall in Paris. He was out of breath, but a mischievous smile played on his lips. He could not afford to rest. The day's events were almost over. He edged his way forward to stand near the speaker's microphone. Writers, artists, scholars, and scientists from around the world had gathered in 1949 at the first Congress of Partisans of Peace. One of them was the great Spanish painter Pablo Picasso.

Picasso was first to welcome the stranger with the playful smile. They grinned like children sharing a secret. Picasso had worked hard to bring his guest to the peace conference. He listened eagerly to the chairman's surprise announcement: "The man who will speak to you has only been in the hall for a few minutes. You have not yet seen him, for he is a hunted man. . . . He is Pablo Neruda."[1]

**Spanish painter Pablo Picasso (left) welcomes Pablo Neruda to the Congress of Partisans of Peace on April 25, 1949, at Salle Pleyel in Paris, France.**

Silence fell over the hall. Then delegates from nearly every continent rose to their feet with a thundering cheer. Pablo Neruda was alive! He stood before them in good health and good spirits. His smile and his wave were bright symbols of hope for the delegates' cause of world peace.

No official news of Neruda, the renowned poet and statesman of Chile, had been heard for more than a year. Six months earlier, a worried Picasso had given the only public speech of his life, hoping to help his friend. At a peace conference in Poland, he pleaded for the world to find Neruda and make sure he was safe. "I have a friend who should be here with us," said Picasso, "a friend who is one of the best men I have ever met. . . . and one of the greatest poets in the world, Pablo Neruda."[2]

Friends in every country feared that Neruda had been put in prison by the government of Chile. The government had taken away many of the people's freedoms. People like Neruda, who spoke out in protest, had been arrested and were never heard from again. They simply disappeared.

Fortunately, Neruda was a man of great resources. His many friends and admirers in Chile had hidden the beloved poet from the government police. After many months, they managed to smuggle him over the Andes Mountains into Argentina and across the ocean to Europe. The fugitive Neruda had an international "poets' brotherhood" of friends who helped him flee to

**Neruda had to cross the rugged Andes Mountains to escape from Chile, where he was in danger of being imprisoned, or an even worse punishment, because of his political views.**

safety.[3] Once he arrived in Paris, friends like Picasso helped him secure a valid passport and the legal right to stay in France.

Naturally joyful and outgoing, Neruda was delighted to end his year of hiding. At last, he was free to move about in public and enjoy an exciting and beautiful city he loved. On April 25, 1949, the forty-four-year-old Neruda made his triumphant appearance at the Paris peace conference. He stood smiling before a sea of welcoming faces. In his gravelly, riveting voice he said:

> Dear friends . . . if I have arrived a bit late at your meeting, it is due to the difficulties I have had to overcome in order to get here. I bring you the greetings of all the people in distant lands. The political persecution which exists in my country has allowed me to appreciate the fact that human solidarity is greater than all barriers."[4]

Neruda read the audience a poem from his new book, published secretly in Chile. This early edition of *Canto General* (*General Song*), written over the previous ten years, was Neruda's tribute to the Americas. He hoped his *Canto General* would describe and celebrate the history, the land, the life, and the struggles of all the people of the Americas.[5] For Neruda, the struggle for peace and justice in the Americas mirrored the same cause for people in all nations. The love and respect for

## Paris

Paris, capital city of France, has long been a world center of the arts and education. For hundreds of years, artists and writers have flocked to Paris to work, study, and enjoy its beauty and cultural life. Historic buildings, lovely gardens and parks, colorful cafes, theaters, and museums gave Paris its nickname, City of Light. Many important artists, writers, and thinkers of the twentieth century made their homes in Paris, including Pablo Picasso.

P A B L O     N E R U D A

# C A N T O
# G E N E R A L

## I

*LA LAMPARA*
*en la*
**TIERRA**
*(13 a 34)*

Amor America (1400).—Vegeta-
ciones. — Algunas bestias.—
Vienen los pajaros.—Los rios
acuden.—Orinoco.—Amazonas.
—Tequendama.—Bio Bio.—Mi-
nerales.—Los hombres.

## II

*ALTURAS*
*de*
**MACCHU PICCHU**
*(37 a 56)*

## III

*Los*
**CONQUISTADORES**
*(59 a 96)*

Vienen por las islas (1493).—Ahora es Cuba.—
Llegan al mar de Mexico (1519).—Cortes.—
Cholula.—Alvarado.—Guatemala.—Un Obis-
po.—La cabeza en el palo.—Homenaje a Balboa.—
Duerme un soldado.—Ximenez de Quesada (1536).—
Cita de cuervos.—Las agonias.—La linea colorada.—
Elegia.—Las guerras.—Descubridores de Chile.—La tierra
combatiente.—Se unen la tierra y el hombre.—Valdivia (1544).—
Ercilla.—Se entierran las lanzas.—El corazon magallanico (1519)
Despierto de pronto en la noche pensando en el extremo sur.—Recuerdo
la soledad del Estrecho.—Los descubridores aparecen y de ellos no que-
da nada.—Solo se impone la desolacion.—Recuerdo al viejo descubridor.—
Magallanes.—Llega al Pacifico.—Todos han muerto.—A pesar de la ira.

This is the title page for Pablo Neruda's *Canto General*, meaning *General Song*, a collection of poems that celebrate the Americas.

life that rang through Neruda's poetry had made him a champion of human rights to all who knew his work.

His escape to Paris began a new chapter in the poet's life. Already known and loved throughout Latin America, Neruda's poetry would soon reach readers throughout Europe and in English-speaking North America as well.[6] In Paris that year and during his later world travels, he would find new friends and new experiences to enrich his poetry. Like his good friend Picasso, Neruda always had a new creative dream to follow. He never stopped learning and growing in his chosen art.

From his youth in the cold rain forests of southern Chile through years of diplomatic work, travel, and political action, Pablo Neruda wrote poetry. In his vast outpouring of poems, the story of his life unfolds. He said, "If you ask me what my poetry is, I must say, I don't know; but if you ask my poetry, it will tell you who I am!"[7] He hoped to speak to and for all people. Readers have responded to his voice with fascination and love from the very beginning.

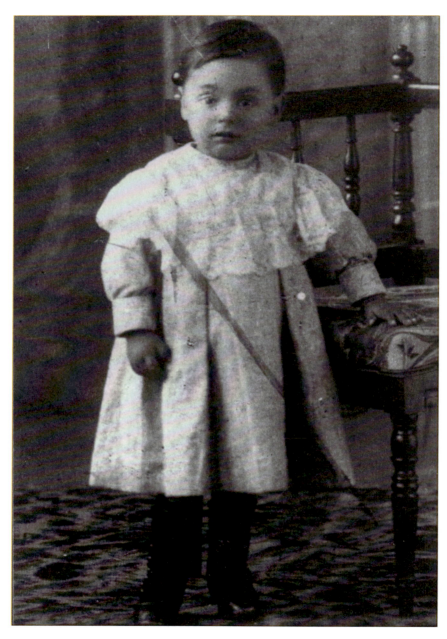

Neruda leans on a chair in this photo of him as a young child.

# 2

# Child of
# the Rain Forest

The boy who would become Pablo Neruda was born on July 12, 1904, in the small country town of Parral in central Chile. His parents named him Ricardo Eliecer Neftalí Reyes Basoalto.[1] They called him Neftalí. His mother, Doña Rosa Basoalto de Reyes, was a teacher. She died of tuberculosis, a lung disease, only a month after Neftalí was born. His father, Don José del Carmen Reyes Morales, was the son of a local farmer. José del Carmen worked at many jobs before finding a successful career as a railroad conductor.

Neftalí lived with his father's parents in Parral until he was two years old. His father then remarried, taking his new wife and Neftalí to live in the village of Temuco, on the edge of the cold rain forests of southern Chile. In 1906, Temuco was a frontier town of rough wooden houses and muddy streets. Settlers from many different countries shared the region with the Mapuche Indians.

Neftalí's new stepmother, Doña Trinidad Candia Marverde, was a kind and loving woman. She took good care of her stepson, but Neftalí was a small, sickly boy in his early years. He later called his stepmother "the guardian angel of my childhood."[2] By the time Neftalí entered school at age six, Doña Trinidad had taught him to read and write. He had already started to explore the natural world around him with curiosity and wonder.

The weather in Temuco was as dramatic as the forests and mountains. All winter, cold rain drummed on the metal roofs of the buildings. From his bedroom window, Neftalí watched the wild wind blow through the trees, sometimes lifting the roof from a neighboring house. "Each house was a ship struggling to make port in the ocean of winter," he wrote later. "The rain was the one unforgettable presence for me then."[3] The sound of rain on the roof competed with the sound of water dripping from endless leaks.

In the hot summers, the roads were filled with dust. In the winter, they were thick with mud. The rain sometimes caused the rivers to flood, washing away houses along the banks. Neftalí remembered struggling to get to school and back in the rain and cold. "The wind snatched our umbrellas away. And the earth shook, trembled."[4] Southern Chile was also a land of frequent earthquakes. Many of the mountains were volcanoes.

Neftalí was fascinated with the rich plant and animal life under the dense towering trees of the rain forest.

**Pablo Neruda grew up in the South American country of Chile. His family moved to Temuco when he was two years old.**

He spent his free time exploring. He collected bird's nests and eggs, spiders, beetles, leaves, ferns, pinecones—whatever small treasures he found. As a friend described Neftalí, "he had an insatiable curiosity for little things (strange stones, pieces of wood, insects). And he never lost that curiosity."[5]

Neftalí also loved the solitary activities of reading and writing. His aunts said that he might look weak but he had a will of iron.[6] A school friend described Neftalí as "very thin, very serious, with an absent-minded expression, arriving late for classes."[7] Another friend, who joined him in exploring the countryside "looking at the world's little things," said Neftalí had a special quality, "a style that belonged only to him and made him different."[8]

## Temperate Rain Forest

West of the Andes Mountains in southern Chile is a cool, wet region known as a temperate rain forest. Like the tropical rain forests near the Equator, these cool forests are home to a rich variety of plants and animals. Many of Chile's rain forest trees, birds, and mammals are found nowhere else on Earth. These include the world's smallest deer and one of the world's largest woodpeckers. This forest is also home to the huge araucaria tree with its dense tangled branches. The araucaria, or monkey puzzle tree, is the world's oldest type of tree, first appearing on earth about 200 million years ago.

He was never much interested in the sports and games the other boys played. Neftalí always lost the acorn fights they had. He enjoyed watching the acorns fly through the air so much that he forgot to dodge the ones that rained down on him. "While I was busy examining the marvelous acorn, green and polished, with its gray wrinkled hood . . . a downpour of acorns would pelt my head," he wrote.[9]

Neftalí's father, José del Carmen, worked as the conductor of a train that carried sand and rocks. The region's heavy rain washed away the soil that held up the railroad tracks. Crews of men worked constantly to build up the land under the tracks. His father some-times took Neftalí out of school and brought him along on overnight train trips. On these trips, while the workers collected the materials they needed, Neftalí was free to explore the forest. His father—a stern, hardworking man—hoped to interest his son in the practical world and lure him away from his constant reading and writing.

By age ten, Neftalí knew he wanted to be a poet, something his father would never approve. "I was not yet writing verse," he later wrote, "but I was already a poet."[10] His love of nature and the wonder he felt in the forest inspired him to write. Later, he described himself as "a remote, shy, solitary witness, clinging to the wall like lichen. I suspect that no one heard me and that very few saw me."[11]

Neftalí spent his evenings writing in his school

notebooks and reading whatever books he could find. Novels by Russian authors Tolstoy and Dostoyevsky, poetry by Frenchmen Rimbaud and Baudelaire, adventure stories by Jules Verne, and the Spanish classic *Don Quixote* were some of his favorites. Through books, he traveled the world and discovered its wonders. He later recalled, "The sack of human wisdom had broken open. . . . Reading, I didn't sleep or eat."[12]

One hot summer, Neftalí's family went to spend a month with friends living near the ocean. The family

> **"Reading, I didn't sleep or eat."**

packed most of their household goods for the trip, including the mattresses to sleep on. Neftalí, his older stepbrother, Rodolfo; and his younger half-sister, Laura, set out with their parents for the journey to the sea. They traveled west by train and riverboat to the coastal town of Puerto Saavedra, where they could hear the ocean waves pounding. Neftalí found himself "overwhelmed" by his first sight of the ocean. The white-capped waves sounded to him like "the loud pounding of a gigantic heart, the heartbeat of the universe."[13] His father insisted that Neftalí and Laura go out in the ocean every day. They were terrified of the rough, icy water and held hands tightly while the waves crashed around them.

During this first visit to the sea, Neftalí learned to ride horses. He enjoyed galloping along the shore. Because he lived in the southern hemisphere, Neftalí's

July birthdays fell during the bitter Temuco winter. To escape the hot, scorching summers in Temuco, his family made many more trips to the ocean in the summer months of January and February. Exploring the land suited Neftalí well. He later wrote about those times: "Along endless beaches or thicketed hills, a communion was started between my spirit—that is, my poetry—and the loneliest land in the world. This was many years ago, but that communion, that revelation, that pact with the wilderness, is still a part of my life."[14] At Puerto Saavedra, Neftalí first saw penguins, wild swans, and flocks of pink flamingos in flight.[15]

Another happy memory of summers in Puerto Saavedra was the small public library Neftalí discovered there. Neftalí remembered the librarian as "a small, white-bearded wizard, the poet Don Augusto Winter." Winter was impressed with Neftalí's love of reading and suggested many new books for his enjoyment. "I would settle myself there [in the library]," Neftalí later wrote, "as if sentenced to read in the three summer months all the books written through the long winters of the world."[16] Neftalí described himself as an ostrich who "gobbled up everything. . . . My appetite for reading did not let up day or night."[17]

When Neftalí was fifteen years old, he met a famous Chilean poet, Gabriela Mistral. She came to Temuco as principal of the local girls' school. Neftalí later wrote that he was scared of this tall woman in long dresses when he visited her several times, but "found her to be very gracious. In her dark face . . . her very white teeth flashed in a full, generous smile that lit up the room."[18] Mistral encouraged Neftalí in his writing and gave him books to read. In 1945, Gabriela Mistral became the first South American to win the Nobel Prize for Literature.

Neftalí later remembered his first poem as one written to his "angelic stepmother whose gentle shadow watched over my childhood."[19] He was almost eleven years old. He tried to show the poem to his parents while they were deep in conversation. His father looked at the poem and said, "Where did you copy that from?"[20] Neftalí had not copied it, but Don José had no patience with his son's love of writing.

Neftalí had better luck with another writing task he attempted. The boys at school would not have been impressed with Neftalí's desire to write poetry, but one of them did ask him to write love letters for him. "I don't remember what these letters were like exactly," Neftalí later wrote, "but they may have been my first literary achievement." When the truth came out that Neftalí was writing the love letters, the girl receiving them gave him a quince, a type of fruit. He kept writing the letters on his own behalf and kept receiving quinces.[21]

Neftalí had a relative in Temuco who offered him his first chance to publish his writing. Orlando Mason was editor of the newspaper *La Mañana*. Mason was also a poet and was an important role model to Neftalí. Mason

Gabriela Mistral was a big influence on Pablo Neruda and later became his friend. Mistral was the name she used as a writer; her real name was Lucila Godoy Alcayaga.

gave poetry readings and was a champion for social justice, especially in defense of the local native people. When he was thirteen years old, Neftalí wrote an essay, which appeared in *La Mañana*. His essay encouraged

> **He pursued his desire to be a poet.**

people to follow their desires with enthusiasm and persistence. He was taking his own advice as he pursued his desire to be a poet.

Neftalí began sending his poems to a larger audience in Chile's capital city of Santiago. In late 1918 and early 1919, sixteen of them were published in the Santiago magazine *Corre Vuela*. His poems were signed "Neftalí Reyes." His father increased his efforts to keep Neftalí from writing poetry. One night, an angry José del Carmen stormed into Neftalí's bedroom, tossed his son's notebooks out the window, and burned them on the patio below.[22]

When he was sixteen years old, Neftalí decided to spare his father the knowledge that he was writing poetry. In October 1920, he began using the pen name "Pablo Neruda" to sign his poems. The pen name soon became Neftalí's new identity. Years later, when asked where he got the name Pablo Neruda, he said he chose the name Neruda from a magazine. He said he did not realize it was the name of a famous Czech writer, Jan Neruda.[23] He never explained his choice of the name Pablo, the Spanish version of Paul.

In March 1921, Neftalí Reyes, the young man who now called himself Pablo Neruda, left his childhood home in Temuco. His father had agreed to support him as a student at the Pedagogical Institute in Santiago. Neftalí agreed to study French and become a language teacher. In José del Carmen's eyes, teaching was a respectable career, unlike writing poetry for a living. At age sixteen, Pablo Neruda said good-bye to the country landscape he had known and loved and boarded the night train for Santiago and a new life. Neruda described the birth of his writing life in these lines from "Poetry":

> *And it was at that age . . . poetry arrived*
> *in search of me. I don't know, I don't know where*
> *it came from, from winter or a river.*
> *I don't know how or when,*
> *no, they were not voices, they were not*
> *words, not silence,*
> *but from a street it called me,*
> *from the branches of night, . . .*
> *And I, tiny being,*
> *drunk with the great starry*
> *void,*
> *likeness, image of*
> *mystery,*
> *felt myself a pure part*
> *of the abyss.*
> *I wheeled with the stars,*
> *My heart broke loose with the wind.*[24]

**Pablo Neruda attended the Pedagogical Institute in Santiago, Chile. Above is a picture of present-day Santiago.**

# Santiago Student Poet

Pablo Neruda's journey to Santiago took him far from the rain forests of his childhood. Snow-capped mountains surrounded Chile's capital city. Adobe buildings and poplar trees replaced the wooden houses and tall oaks and araucaria trees of Temuco. As he stepped off the train, Neruda entered a new world of independence and freedom. He was far from his father's disapproving eye. He could read and write whenever and for as long as he wanted. He wrote later that he arrived in Santiago with his "head filled with books, dreams, and poems buzzing around like bees."[1]

Like most university students, Neruda lived in a boardinghouse. With his small allowance from home, he was poor and often hungry. He said, "I wrote a lot more than I had up until then, but I ate a lot less."[2] He dressed in a black suit, a wide-brimmed black hat, and a long cape his father had given him. The cape was

**Pablo Neruda often dressed in a black hat, a suit, and a cape that his father had given him.**

designed to keep railroad men warm as they worked outside in the harsh winter. For Neruda, it became a symbol of his new life as a poet.[3]

The school year began in March, at the end of summer in Chile. Neruda enrolled at the university to major in French. He soon began spending more time writing poems than studying for his classes. He found a group of friends who shared his love of books and poetry. They spent their evenings together talking far into the night. "Conversations and poems were passed around till daybreak," he later wrote.[4] The friends had a common bond. Most were students who were poor and often hungry. Neruda spent his days reading and writing in his room. He finished several poems each day and drank endless cups of tea, a substitute for food when he could not afford to eat.

Times were bad for the average citizen of Chile in the early 1920s. After World War I, the country entered a time of economic depression. During the war years, 1914 to 1918, the economy of Chile had thrived. A large market for mining goods—copper and nitrate—from the Atacama Desert in northern Chile provided jobs for many and created fortunes for wealthy investors. With the end of the war, demand for these products fell. Workers were left unemployed and hungry. Many migrated south to the capital city to look for jobs. They looked to the government for help with job opportunities and fair treatment. In 1918 and 1919, protest rallies and strikes brought violent clashes between workers and government forces.

## Atacama Desert

The Atacama of northern Chile is one of the world's oldest and driest deserts. It averages less than one-half inch of rain each year. The Atacama is a barren region with almost no plant life, but it contains huge deposits of valuable minerals. The Atacama is rich in copper. It is also the world's only source of natural sodium nitrate, a mineral used for fertilizer and explosives. People have lived in this harsh landscape for about ten thousand years. Because the Atacama is so dry, the artifacts of its ancient people are still in excellent condition. The world's oldest mummies have been found there.

Students at the university raised their voices in support of the workers. Neruda spent much of his time at the student federation headquarters. Student leaders spoke out for political reform, social justice, a more equal distribution of the country's wealth, and economic opportunity. Student attempts to criticize the government were often met with violence. While still in Temuco, Neruda had learned of a student rebellion that was crushed by the government. Government destruction of the student federation headquarters and the killing of a student poet deeply disturbed Neruda.[5]

Neruda had published poems in the student magazine *Claridad* even before he arrived in Santiago. As a university student, he began spending his afternoons at the office of the *Claridad*. He published poems and a political column for the magazine. To make a little money, he worked on translations and wrote articles for other magazines and newspapers.

Before long, Neruda lost his small allowance from home when his father found out he was writing poems instead of studying. A little money still came now and then. His stepmother smuggled some to the starving poet through his younger half sister Laura. Neruda was a leader among his fellow writers and artists. They admired his poetry as well as his friendly manner and easy laughter. Women liked him very much. He was often seen in the evening walking on the boulevard arm-in-arm with a woman.

**Pablo Neruda (left) works with a friend, Alberto Rojas Jiménez, in the *Claridad* office.**

Neruda moved from one boardinghouse to another. He sometimes lived with friends and sometimes alone. Neruda was looking for better places to live with little money to pay for them. He carried along his small collection of books and his few clothes.

He spent his days in his room writing. A friend wrote of visiting Neruda in his room and talking to him as the poet continued to write. "Pablo went on writing and spoke to me from time to time. . . . It seems that not only did it not disturb him to have someone next to him interrupting his work—he enjoyed it. Rather than getting in the way, it appeared to help him."[6] During his student days, Neruda discovered the joy of having like-minded friends around him as much as possible.

In 1923, when Neruda was nineteen years old, he had a collection of poems ready for his first book. The Chilean student federation published *Crepusculario* (*Twilight Book*). Neruda had to raise the money himself to pay for the printing. He sold a few pieces of furniture, pawned the watch his father had given him, and even parted with his black suit.[7] *Crepusculario*, a name Neruda came up with, contained forty-eight poems, some written when he was still living in Temuco. The poems were filled with themes of sadness, melancholy, and love. Neruda later wrote that he spent many hours watching sunsets and the coming of twilight on the balcony of his boardinghouse in his early student days.[8]

In June 1924, just before his twentieth birthday, Neruda published another book of poetry that would make him famous throughout Latin America. *Viente Poemas de Amor y una Cancíon Desesperada* (*Twenty Love Songs and a Song of Despair*) was immediately popular with readers, who learned many of the verses by heart. These love poems "became engraved on the minds and on the lips of readers throughout Chile, and later the whole of the Spanish-speaking world, and remain so to this day."[9]

Neruda said the inspiration for these poems came from his love of the natural world of southern Chile and his experiences as a student and writer in the artistic community in Santiago.[10] One friend from that time said that Neruda's two books of poetry quickly earned him "the greatest fame ever witnessed in Chile."[11]

Readers loved Neruda's poetry for its heartfelt emotion that they could share. Literary critics admired it, too. Neruda became a celebrity overnight.

Unfortunately, Neruda's instant fame did not bring much money. He remained a starving poet. He spent his days reading great works of literature and writing his poetry without much financial reward. By the age of twenty-two, he had published two successful books of poetry, 108 articles in *Claridad*, and many book reviews and literary articles in magazines and newspapers. Neruda continued to join his friends in their long evenings of talk and laughter, but they sensed he was longing to leave Chile and travel to other parts of the world.[12]

> **Neruda's instant fame did not bring much money.**

When he could, Neruda accepted invitations to visit new places in Chile. He went home for summer trips to the beach at Puerto Saavedra with his family. He visited a friend who was teaching Spanish in Ancud, located on a beautiful island in southern Chile. When he was with his family, Neruda continued to argue with his father over his writing career. Despite his son's fame, José del Carmen still insisted he was wasting his life trying to be a poet. In fact, Neruda still depended on his stepmother for money to buy food. Neruda also made several visits to the beautiful port city of Valparaíso, on the Pacific coast near Santiago. He wrote, "Santiago is a captive city behind walls of snow. Valparaíso . . . throws open its

**A young Pablo Neruda poses with his sister, Laura.**

doors wide to the infinite sea, to its street cries, to the eyes of children."[13]

Neruda knew his considerable accomplishments could not provide him with a decent living in Chile. His friends expected a young man with his literary achievements to travel to Europe, specifically to Paris, the world capital of cultural life. Neruda recalled people asking, "Well, what are you doing here? You must go to Paris."[14] Like many artists and writers in Latin America, Neruda applied for a job representing the government. Jobs in the foreign service were a way for the government to support the arts. Work as a foreign consul, or diplomat, carried few responsibilities and left writers time to pursue their literary art.

With the help of a wealthy friend, Neruda applied to Chile's foreign minister for work as a diplomat. The minister read Neruda a list of vacant positions overseas. Neruda listened to the names of countries all over the world. "I managed to catch only one name, which I had never heard or read before: Rangoon."[15] When the Minister asked where he wanted to go, Neruda replied with the only name he could remember, "Rangoon." He had no idea where or what it was. Rangoon was the capital city of Burma, now called Myanmar, a country in Southeast Asia. When Neruda's friends came to celebrate his new job, he had forgotten the name of the city and could only tell them that he was bound for Asia.

At a farewell party in Valparaíso, Neruda met an old friend, Alvaro Hinojosa, who made him an attractive offer. If Neruda exchanged his first-class boat ticket for two third-class tickets, his friend could come along, too. Neruda liked Hinojosa. His friend had some experience with foreign travel, which might be very useful since Neruda had none. Neither traveler had much money. Together they boarded the train that would take them over the Andes Mountains to Argentina and on to the Atlantic coast. On June 18, 1927, just before Neruda's twenty-third birthday, he and Hinojosa boarded a German steamship bound for Lisbon, Portugal. Their journey to the far side of the earth—and unexpected adventure—had begun.

# 4

# Diplomat East and West

Neruda celebrated his birthday just before his ship landed in Portugal. As usual, he worried about money. He had heard stories during the voyage about the high cost of living in Asia. There were also reports of the many tropical diseases he would face. "But what is there to do?" he asked in a letter to his sister, Laura. "We have to submit to life and struggle with it."[1]

From Portugal, Neruda and Hinojosa traveled to Spain and farther north to France. In Paris, Neruda hoped to meet the famous French poets whose work he admired. Instead, he found a friendly circle of Latin American writers who welcomed him. Traveling south to the French port city of Marseilles, Neruda and Hinojosa caught a ship to continue their journey east. Neruda wrote stories about the trip and sent them home to the Santiago daily newspaper *La Nación*. The two friends sailed east across the Mediterranean Sea to Port Said,

Egypt, for the passage through the Suez Canal. They reached their destination in Singapore in October 1927, four months after leaving South America.

Many adventures awaited Neruda as he learned the ways of diplomacy and the geography of the Far East. In Singapore, Neruda wrote, "We thought we were next door to Rangoon. What a bitter letdown! What had only been a few millimeters on the map had become a gaping abyss."[2] The Chilean consul in Singapore told Neruda and his friend that they had just missed the boat that could take them to Rangoon. Even worse, there were no funds waiting for them in Singapore. Completely out of money, the two young men had to borrow from the consul to survive the next few days until the boat to Rangoon returned.

At the end of October 1927, they finally reached Rangoon, Burma. In 1927, Burma was part of the British colony of India. Neruda's life in the diplomatic service got off to a very confusing start. He had to find his own housing in an unfamiliar city. His duties as consul from Chile were as small as his salary. "My official duties demanded my attention only once every three months, when a ship arrived . . . bound for Chile with hard paraffin and large cases of tea," he wrote.[3] Once he had stamped and signed papers for the ship, his duties were complete for another three months.

Neruda was lonely and restless. He missed the artistic and literary friends who laughed and talked into the night with him in Chile. He missed being surrounded

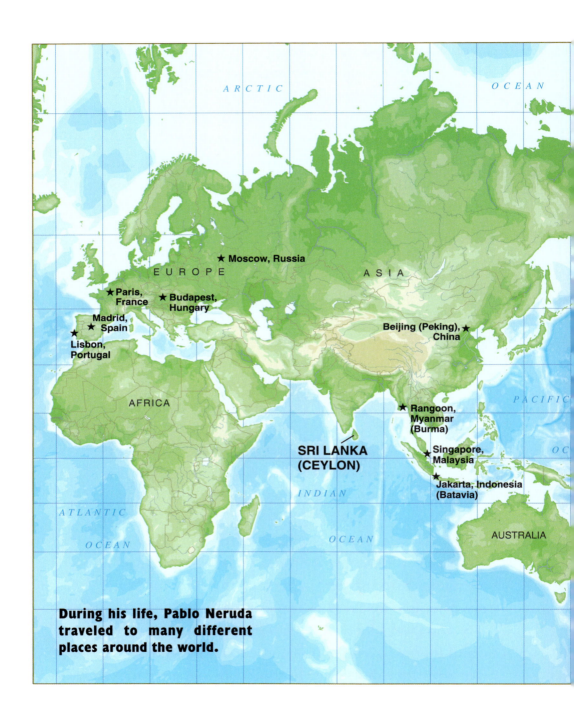

★ Moscow, Russia

EUROPE

ASIA

★ Paris, France

★ Budapest, Hungary

Madrid, ★ Spain

Beijing (Peking), ★ China

★ Lisbon, Portugal

AFRICA

★ Rangoon, Myanmar (Burma)

SRI LANKA (CEYLON)

★ Singapore, Malaysia

★ Jakarta, Indonesia (Batavia)

AUSTRALIA

ARCTIC          OCEAN

PACIFIC

ATLANTIC

OCEAN

INDIAN

OCEAN

**During his life, Pablo Neruda traveled to many different places around the world.**

by the musical rhythms of the Spanish language. He had little knowledge of spoken English. He felt left out of the social world of the British diplomats around him in Rangoon. Neruda could not speak Burmese either, but he felt more comfortable with the people in the busy streets and marketplaces. Unfortunately, mingling with the Burmese was frowned upon by British society. Neruda found himself caught between two worlds. "These two worlds never touched," he wrote. "The natives were not allowed in the places reserved for the English, and the English lived away from the throbbing pulse of the country."[4]

Feeling depressed and alone, Neruda wrote little poetry during this time. He thought about leaving the diplomatic service and moving to Europe. He complained in a letter to his sister about the terrible heat, both day and night: "Life in Rangoon is a terrible exile. . . . So, what am I going to live on in Europe? I could eat and live there with very little money, but where am I going to get that little money? Everything's difficult for me, and I feel tired and ill."[5] Alvaro Hinojosa, Neruda's only friend in Burma, had decided to travel on to India.

In April 1928, Neruda began a love affair with a beautiful Burmese woman who worked in an office in Rangoon. He called her Josie Bliss. Living with a Burmese woman made Neruda even more of an exile from the British community in Rangoon. In time, he grew frightened of Bliss's jealous nature. She said that only if he died would she stop fearing that he would

**Pablo Neruda rests on a beach in Rangoon, Burma, with a local man. Today, Burma is called Myanmar.**

leave her.[6] When Neruda learned that the government of Chile was transferring him, he decided to leave Burma secretly without Bliss.

Neruda wrote to his family that he was moving to the city of Colombo, on the island of Ceylon (today Sri Lanka), south of India. "I'll have the same salary as in Rangoon, and the climate there is just as bad, or even worse . . . but it was becoming unbearable and tiring for me to live in the same place for so long, and I accept my transfer with joy."[7] He sailed for his new post with hope for a fresh and happier beginning.

When he arrived in Colombo, Neruda found a small cottage by the sea. He wrote to his stepmother that the new place reminded him of Puerto Saavedra, the Chilean seaside town where he spent many happy days during his childhood.[8] His job as Chilean consul in Ceylon was much the same as it had been in Burma. Once again, he felt that he belonged neither with the ruling British diplomats nor the native people of the island. Neruda wrote, "I had only solitude open to me, so that time was the loneliest in my life."[9]

He woke up early each morning and walked on the beach, practiced his swimming, and returned home to eat lunch and work. His only companions were a dog, a tame mongoose named Kiria, and Brampy, a servant boy who never spoke. Neruda spent his time reading the many books in English that were available in Ceylon. He wrote poetry and hoped that a publisher in Spain would

Since Sri Lanka is a tropical island nation, it has many scenic beaches. Sri Lanka, another country where Neruda worked for the Chilean government, was once called Ceylon.

## Pablo's Mongoose

Pablo Neruda loved animals. He had enjoyed watching them in the forests of his childhood. He visited every city zoo he discovered in his travels. Among his more unusual pets was the mongoose he adopted in Ceylon. A mongoose is about sixteen inches long with stiff gray-yellow fur, a native of Africa and southern Asia. It has a fierce nature, but it can be tamed. Known for its ability to kill snakes, the mongoose is lightning fast. Neruda's mongoose, Kiria, had only one encounter with a snake. Surprisingly, she ran at top speed in the opposite direction!

soon accept his new book of poems, *Residencia en la Tierra* (*Residence on Earth*).

In February 1930, Neruda learned that the diplomatic service was transferring him once again. This time his new post, on the island of Singapore, would be busier and more exciting. He decided to bring along his servant, Brampy, and also to smuggle Kiria the mongoose on board the ship to Singapore. When they arrived, Neruda found a hotel room and handed over his laundry to be washed. Then he found out that his new post was actually on another island in the Dutch colonial city of Batavia (now Jakarta). The last ship for Batavia was about to sail. Brampy ran off to collect Neruda's wet clothes, and they hurried to back to the harbor.[10]

While Neruda was staying in a hotel in Batavia, his pet mongoose escaped and was never seen again.

Brampy disappeared, too. "My solitude became even deeper," Neruda wrote.[11] Soon, Neruda moved into his official government house and took up his new post, a higher-level job with a better salary than he had before.

During the summer of 1930, Neruda met a young Dutch woman named Maria Antonieta Hagenaar Vogelzang. He wrote, "She was a tall, gentle girl and knew nothing of the world of arts and letters."[12] Vogelzang was thirty years old, and Neruda was twenty-six. Neruda called her Maruca, his version of her Dutch nickname, Maryka. They were married on December 6, 1930. Neruda did not speak Dutch, and Maruca did not speak Spanish, but they each knew a little English.

Neruda wrote home to his family in Chile, "From now on, you will no longer have to be concerned that your son is alone and far from you, since I have some-one who is with me. . . . We are poor, but happy."[13] In March 1931, Neruda's salary was cut in half. Chile's economy was suffering from the effects of the worldwide depression that followed the 1929 stock market crash. At the beginning of 1932, Neruda's post as consul of Singapore and Batavia was eliminated. He and his new wife returned to Chile. His five-year period in Asia was over.

Neruda had written home during these years that his "only territory, his only certainty . . . was the Spanish language."[14] The young couple spent two months at sea as they traveled south along the coast of Africa, across the Atlantic and around Cape Horn. They landed at the city of Puerto Montt on the southern tip of Chile. A train took them through the rainy autumn weather of April to Temuco and a reunion with Neruda's family.

Neruda and his wife spent only a brief time in Temuco before heading to Santiago. Neruda's father still disapproved of him. The poet had returned home to Chile with no job, no money, and a wife to support who did not speak Spanish. Neruda had returned to a country still suffering from economic and political unrest.

Chile's capital city was in turmoil. A new leader, President Carlos Dávila, had just come to power following the overthrow of right-wing dictator Carlos Ibáñez. Neruda found some things unchanged in Santiago. His old circle of friends from his student days welcomed him back to their life of late nights and long conversations. Neruda was married now, but he and his wife did not share many interests. Maruca did not go out with him to local bars and cafes or join in her husband's active social life.

Friends helped Neruda get a part-time job in the library of the foreign ministry. His small salary barely allowed him to live. His finances were in a bad state, but Neruda's fame as a poet continued to grow. He gave a reading of his work in Santiago on May 11, 1932, to a large crowd of devoted fans. He was still seeking a publisher for his book *Residencia en la Tierra*. He had hoped to publish the book outside of Chile because of the terrible state of the country's economy. His country's poverty had ended his diplomatic career. Now he struggled to get his poetry published for the very same reason.

At last, in February 1933, a special edition of one hundred copies of *Residencia en la Tierra* was published. The large-size luxury edition was too expensive for many people to buy, but the book Neruda had worked on for five years was finally in print. One reviewer noted the deep appeal of Neruda's poetry for his readers: "The voice of Pablo Neruda has influenced a whole generation in Chile and has even sounded out among other people far from America."[15]

In August 1933, the twenty-nine-year-old Neruda received welcome news. He had been appointed to a new job as Chilean consul in Buenos Aires, the capital of neighboring Argentina. Life in Santiago had become very expensive. Opportunities to earn a living were scarce. Neruda was relieved to find work elsewhere.

> *The book Neruda had worked on for five years was finally in print.*

The move to Buenos Aires was very different from Neruda's move to the lonely isolation of Burma. He quickly formed a new circle of friends among the writers of the Argentine capital. One friend who became very important to him was the visiting Spanish poet and playwright Federico García Lorca, in Argentina for the opening of his play *Blood Wedding*. They admired each other's work. Lorca signed a copy of his book *Gypsy Ballads* and presented it to Neruda: "For my dear Pablo, one of the few great poets I've had the good fortune to love and know."[16]

Neruda spent eight months in Buenos Aires before a new and more important opportunity came his way. He had spent his time in Argentina reading, writing, and enjoying the company of friends. Soon he would move into a larger world to face some of the greatest challenges of his life. For many years, he had wished for a chance to live in Spain. Now Neruda had a new diplomatic assignment overseas. In May 1934, he and Maruca boarded a ship for the Spanish port city of Barcelona. Despite their unhappy relationship, Maruca was eagerly expecting their first child.

# 5

# Closer to Blood Than to Ink

After a three-week voyage across the Atlantic, Neruda and his wife arrived in Barcelona on the Mediterranean coast of Spain. Here, the poet took up his new position as Chilean consul. Barcelona was a beautiful city, but Neruda soon found himself longing to be closer to the heart of Spanish literary activity. A friend had told him, "Pablo, you should go live in Madrid. That's where the poetry is."[1] At that time, another famous poet from Chile served as consul in Madrid, Gabriela Mistral whom Neruda had met when he was a schoolboy in Temuco.

Neruda decided to visit Madrid, Spain's capital, in June 1934. Federico García Lorca was now back home in Spain. Lorca welcomed Neruda at the Madrid train station. Neruda soon found himself at the center of an exciting circle of writers who knew and admired his work. "Within a few days," he wrote, "I was one with the

Spanish poets. . . . The Spaniards of my generation were more brotherly, closer-knit and better-spirited than their counterparts in Latin America."[2]

Neruda's wife soon followed him to Madrid. They settled into a home they called the Casa de las Flores (House of Flowers), made by combining two small apartments. The apartment was always open to friends who wanted to join him for drink, food, or literary conversation any time of the day or night.[3] García Lorca and Neruda were always together. Neruda often visited García Lorca's theater rehearsals. Neruda wrote that García Lorca "was the most loved, the most cherished, of all Spanish poets, and he was the closest to being a child, because of his marvelous happy temperament."[4]

On December 6, 1934, at a lecture at the University of Madrid, García Lorca introduced Neruda as one of the greatest of all Latin American poets. García Lorca told listeners that Neruda's poetry was "closer to blood than to ink."[5] He admired Neruda's power to reach the heart of human emotion and move closer to life than words "ink" would normally allow. In the spring of 1935, Neruda wrote a poem praising his friend, "Oda a Federico García Lorca."

While he worked, wrote, and celebrated life with his friends, Neruda had a heavy weight on his heart. In August 1934, his wife had given birth to their daughter, Malva Marina. The baby had been born seriously ill. Her survival was in doubt during her early months.

Neruda watched helplessly as his daughter failed to grow and develop normally. After her first year and a half, she was diagnosed with a condition called hydrocephaly, an enlarged head caused by fluid around the brain. Doctors at that time had no treatment for the condition. Neruda and his wife continued to hope that their child's health would improve.

Each afternoon, Neruda and his friends gathered to discuss their plans for the evening. The talk often centered on Spain's political troubles. Neruda said to a friend when he first arrived in Madrid, "I don't know anything about politics."[6] Even though he worked in the government service, Neruda simply did his job as consul—paperwork and communication. His real work was his writing. Until his years in Spain, he had stood back from the political conflicts that were now becoming more and more threatening.

> **"I don't know anything about politics."**

Spain in 1935 was on the brink of a civil war. The worldwide depression caused terrible economic suffering for the poorest citizens. They looked to the government for some action to improve their lives. Throughout its history, Spain had been a monarchy, ruled by kings and queens. Pressure for change and greater social justice led to the end of the monarchy. Spain then established a republic, a form of democratic government.

The resignation of Spain's King Alfonso XIII divided the country into different camps. Some wanted the return of the monarchy and an end to government reforms. Some wanted greater reforms and a more democratic government. Still others wanted no central government and to turn factories over to the workers. Neruda's friends sided with the Popular Front, the supporters of the new republican form of government. The possibility of a violent clash between the various forces grew as the months passed.

Neruda and Mistral decided to exchange consul positions. Neruda stayed in Madrid, and Mistral moved to Lisbon, capital of Portugal. Madrid was the center for support of the Popular Front. Neruda's wife and child went back to Barcelona on Spain's eastern coast. They would be safer there from the dangers of political unrest. Neruda tried to stay busy with his writing. He also worked on Spanish translations of the work of English poet William Blake (1757–1827).

One friend Neruda saw often in Madrid was Delia del Carril, a painter from Argentina who had lived in Paris for many years. Del Carril was a beautiful, bright, and political woman, who was twenty years older than Neruda. He came to admire and love her. She was nick-named "La Hormiguita" (Little Ant) for her bustling energy. During her years in Paris, she had become a devoted Communist.

Neruda knew he could no longer stand back and merely watch. A terrible struggle was about to engulf the

Spanish people, especially the poor. On July 17, 1936, carefully timed military revolts broke out throughout Spain and the Spanish colony of Morocco. General Francisco Franco became leader of the forces fighting against the Popular Front republican government for control of Spain. The conflict, called the Spanish Civil War, began that summer and would last for the next three years.

Neruda's good friend Federico García Lorca was captured and executed by Franco's Nationalist rebels. Lorca had returned to his home province of Andalusia in southern Spain for safety. The news of Lorca's death drove Neruda to announce his support of the

## Beyond the Borders

The world was watching in 1936 when Spanish army units rebelled against the government of Spain. Countries outside Spain soon became involved. Nazi Germany and Fascist Italy bombed Spanish cities on behalf of the rebel forces of General Franco. The Soviet Union sent supplies to support the Spanish government. In the United States and more than fifty other countries, people joined international brigades to help defend the Spanish government. More than fifty-nine thousand people volunteered to fight. They believed it was a fight for freedom. Famous Americans, including the writer Ernest Hemingway, went to Spain during the civil war. Thousands of foreign volunteers were killed during the conflict. Franco's forces won in March 1939.

Republican cause. "And so the Spanish war, which changed my poetry, began for me with a poet's disappearance," he wrote.[7] With the death of his friend, Neruda committed himself to the cause of social and political justice. In the future, he would use his poetry not only to express personal feelings but to speak out against suffering and injustice.

He began writing his poetic work *España en el Corazón* (*Spain in the Heart*). It would become his tribute to the victims of the Spanish Civil War. With the first public reading of a poem called "Song of the Mothers of Dead Militiamen," Neruda revealed his new political stand. As a diplomat, he was expected not to take sides in the Spanish Civil War. By speaking openly about his political beliefs, he put himself in danger of losing his job.

> *"The Spanish war . . . began for me with a poet's disappearance."*

By November 1936, the forces of General Franco were threatening the capital city. It was time to leave Madrid. Neruda and his companions traveled to Barcelona. There, he, his wife, and his daughter boarded a train to safety in France. Neruda found a residence for his wife and child near a medical clinic in the seaside resort of Monte Carlo. He traveled on to Paris by himself.

In Paris, Neruda joined a group of writers and kept busy with projects in support of the Spanish Republic. At the beginning of 1937, his friend Delia del Carril

came to meet him in Paris. They began a love affair.
Del Carril had many friends among the writers and
artists of Paris. She introduced Neruda to writers who
became his good friends, including the French
Communist poets Paul Eluard and Louis Aragon. In
January, Neruda gave a speech honoring the memory of
Federico García Lorca. In his talk, he promised to work
for social justice and the welfare of the common working
people whose lives were being destroyed by war.[8]

The government of Chile closed the consulate in
Madrid and cut off Neruda's income. "My consular
duties had come to an end," he wrote, "because I had
taken part in the defense of the Spanish Republic."[9]
Chile was officially neutral, not taking sides in the war.
The loss of his income left Neruda without enough
money to support Maruca and Malva Marina. Without
money to live on, Maruca decided to leave France and
return to her family home in the Netherlands. Neruda
never saw her or their child again.[10]

In Paris, Neruda scraped by on the little money
he could earn. He worked for the committee for the
defense of culture in Paris. "For months, we ate very
little and badly," he wrote.[11] In July 1937, Neruda
returned to Spain to attend a writers' congress that he
had helped organize. Famous writers from around the
world were invited to show support for the Spanish
Republican cause. A train left Paris bound for Valencia
and then Madrid. About two hundred writers from thirty countries came to Spain to attend the conference.

Pablo Neruda and Delia del Carrill look into each other's eyes on the grounds of his home Isla Negra near Valparaíso, Chile, in 1939.

While in Madrid, Neruda returned to his apartment in the Casa de las Flores. He found the roof blown off and the walls damaged by gunfire. All his books and other possessions lay scattered on the floor. He decided to walk away and save nothing from the rubble, not even his books. The scenes of destruction in Madrid seemed too unreal to believe or understand. "War is as whimsical as dreams," he wrote.[12]

Neruda and Delia del Carril left Europe to return to Chile in October 1937. In Santiago, they found a comfortable house to share. It soon became a gathering place where friends were always welcome. In November, the first edition of *España en el Corazón* was published with photos. Del Carril went home to Argentina to visit her family. Neruda traveled throughout Chile giving public readings of his poetry and raising funds to help victims of the Spanish Civil War. He began thinking of his audience not as a gathering of literary friends, but as the ordinary working people of the world. He discovered a new desire to reach out to them and touch their hearts with his poetry.[13] He began to use his poetry as a voice for social justice.

In the late 1930s, the forces of fascism were rising in Europe. The Nazi Party gained power in Germany. Chile and other countries had many citizens who were sympathetic to the Nazis. By taking sides against the Spanish fascist forces, Neruda made himself unpopular with some groups in Chile. At the same time, Neruda faced two personal losses—in 1938 his father's death in May and the death of his beloved stepmother in August.

Neruda went back to his childhood home in Temuco twice to attend the funeral services. Traveling by train, he thought of his father and remembered the train trips of his childhood. His parents and the rainy landscape had formed his life. Memories of his childhood, of his stern, hardworking father, and of his kind, loving mother would always be part of his poetry.

Neruda began using his poetry readings to support a political campaign. He wanted to help elect Pedro Aguirre Cerda, the presidential candidate of the Popular Front. Chile's Radical Socialist and Communist parties joined forces in the Popular Front. Neruda's candidate won the election against great odds. Soon Neruda found himself working for Chile's foreign service once again. He was sent back to Paris as special consul for Spanish emigration.

Neruda's new job was to rescue as many refugees as possible from the Spanish Civil War. More than half a million Spanish Republicans had escaped over the Pyrenees Mountains to France. They were fleeing from the German bombs, the Italian soldiers, and the forces of General Franco. The refugees were living in camps under terrible conditions.

Neruda's work was to fill a ship with Spanish refugee families and bring them back to Chile. In April 1939, he and Delia del Carril arrived in Paris and began to organize and carry out the rescue mission. They had many obstacles to overcome. The French government did little to help with the refugee problem. The government of Chile had little money for the rescue project.

At last, on August 4, 1939, Neruda watched as two thousand Spanish refugees—artists, writers, teachers, farmers, shepherds—boarded the *Winnipeg*, a ship bound for Chile. The passengers endured the hot and crowded one-month voyage across the Atlantic. They sailed through the Panama Canal and down the coast of South America to Chile. It was a voyage to freedom and a proud achievement for Neruda. He wrote, "There were fishermen, peasants, laborers, intellectuals, a cross section of strength, heroism, and hard work. My poetry in its struggle had succeeded in finding them a country. And I was filled with pride."[14] Neruda wanted a life of peace, freedom, and plenty for all the people of the world. In these lines from "The Great Tablecloth," Neruda describes his feelings:

> *Let us sit down soon to eat*
> *with all those who haven't eaten;*
> *let us spread great tablecloths,*
> *put salt in the lakes of the world,*
> *set up planetary bakeries,*
> *tables with strawberries in snow,*
> *and a plate like the moon itself*
> *from which we can all eat.*
> *For now I ask no more*
> *than the justice of eating.*[15]

# All the Americas

The *Winnipeg* with its Spanish refugees arrived in Valparaíso, Chile, on September 3, 1939, just as World War II began in Europe. Neruda remained in France for several more months. With sadness, he watched the French people prepare for war before he returned home to Chile.

In January 1940, he began looking for a quiet place to live and work on his writing. He found a remote stone house south of Valparaíso. The house was known as Isla Negra (Black Island). It overlooked a large black rock just offshore. Isla Negra soon became Neruda's favorite writing place. It was close to the ocean in a beautiful natural setting.

But it was not quite time to settle down to a quiet life of writing. The government of Chile asked Neruda to serve as consul in Mexico City. Neruda felt it was his duty to share in the political life of his country. At the end of July 1940, Neruda and Delia del Carril sailed north from Valparaíso to the Mexican port of Manzanillo. They settled in a large house in Mexico City.

Before long, their house became a welcoming place for the famous artists and writers of Mexico. Refugees from the war in Europe visited, too. Neruda praised Mexico for opening its borders to political refugees. His friend Gabriela Mistral and others helped many people

**One of the homes of Pablo Neruda, Isla Negra, is preserved as a museum today.**

escape from the war in Europe. Many helped as Neruda had done with the passengers of the *Winnipeg*.

Mexico remained neutral during World War II, but talk of the war could be heard everywhere. Mexico was home to people of a wide range of political beliefs. There were supporters of Communism and also those who supported the Nazi Party in Germany. After the tragedy of the Spanish Civil War, Neruda had strong political feelings himself. As a diplomat for Chile, also a neutral country at the time, he was not supposed to take sides openly. But he could not help expressing his beliefs in his speaking and writing. He sometimes found himself in trouble with the governments of both Mexico and Chile.

When he could escape from his duties as Chilean consul, Neruda worked steadily at his poetry. He had an idea for a long poetry collection called *Canto General* (General Song). It would tell the story of the people of Chile. Working in his favorite green ink, Neruda showed each poem he composed to Delia del Carril for her approval. She was a thoughtful critic. Neruda valued her opinion and made any changes she suggested for his work.[1] She spent most of her time entertaining the flood of guests who came to visit, but worked at her painting when she could.

Visitors reported that Neruda filled his home with a large collection of seashells and other objects that reminded him of the sea, "as if he were nostalgic for the coastline of his homeland."[2] Neruda was a passionate shopper. He loved the bright colors and fine crafts of Mexico that he found in the outdoor markets. He wrote:

> Mexico is a land of crimson and phosphorescent turquoise shawls. Mexico is a land of earthen bowls and pitchers, and fruit. . . . The most beautiful markets in the world have all this to offer. Fruit and wool, clay and weaving looms, give evidence of the incredible skill of the fertile and timeless fingers of the Mexicans.[3]

While living in Mexico City, Neruda took every chance to travel around Mexico. He also visited neighboring countries. He traveled to Guatemala where he met the novelist Miguel Angel Asturias, who became a good friend. Neruda also visited Panama, Colombia, and Peru. As he traveled, Neruda gained greater knowledge of the wide variety of landscapes and people to be found in Latin America. He took an interest in the lives of the people and the politics of each region.

> "Mexico is a land of earthen bowls and pitchers, and fruit."

Among the friends Neruda made in Mexico were the great mural painters Diego Rivera, José Clemente Orozco, and David Alfaro Siqueiros. All combined their political beliefs with their artistic work. Like them, Neruda made his personal political beliefs known. He sometimes found himself in conflict with political enemies in Mexico. In December 1941, Neruda and his friends were attacked in a restaurant by a group of Germans who sympathized with the Nazi Party.

Six-year-old Poli Délano, the son of good friends of Neruda, was present on that day. He wrote about the episode years later. He remembered his father pushing him under the restaurant table for safety. Neruda, Delia del Carril, and Poli's parents got into a fight with the party of Germans at the next table. Poli heard glasses breaking and furniture crashing. The battle came to a sudden end when Neruda was struck on the head with a sharp object and began to bleed heavily. "Of course, the Germans disappeared. Tio Pablo (Uncle Pablo) had blood running down his face, and his whole shirt was stained red," Poli wrote.[4] Neruda had to be taken to a nearby hospital, but fortunately his wound was not serious.

In 1942, Neruda made his first visit to Cuba. He enjoyed observing life in this Latin American island nation. Neruda and del Carril explored the beaches and forests and found a wonderful new snail shell to collect. They returned to Mexico City with two suitcases full of *polimyta* shells. Neruda could not resist these brightly colored, striped shells of a large Cuban land snail.[5]

In early 1943, the first few poems of *Canto General* were published in Mexico. At that time, Neruda called the work *Canto General de Chile*. In time, the *General Song of Chile* would grow to become the song of all the people of the Americas. New selections of Neruda's poems were also published in Peru and Colombia that year. In March, sad news arrived for Neruda. His daughter, Malva Marina, had died in the Netherlands at age eight. Within a few months, Neruda had lost several close friends and his only child.

While the war raged on in Europe, Neruda enjoyed life in Mexico, although his work for the consular service was tedious and dull. It also conflicted with his need to express his beliefs freely. "As a writer, my duty is to defend freedom as an absolute norm of the civil and human condition," he wrote.[6] He asked for a six-month leave of absence and prepared to return to Chile.

Neruda received word that a divorce from his first wife had been granted by the Mexican government. Just before his thirty-ninth birthday, he married Delia del Carril at an outdoor ceremony with songs and poetry. They were a happy and devoted couple despite their twenty-year age difference.

During his three-year stay in Mexico, Neruda expanded his knowledge of the history and geography of the Americas. As a poet who loved life, he felt a strong commitment to social and political justice. He wanted to ensure a good life for all people. Neruda wrote that his poetry before *Canto General* was too narrow: "I had probed man's heart; without a thought for mankind."[7]

Through his writing and speaking, Neruda had become a major public figure. Thousands of people attended a farewell tribute for him as he left Mexico. Before returning to Chile, Neruda and his wife traveled throughout Latin America. They visited Panama, Colombia, and Peru. Neruda wanted to see the ancient

Incan city of Machu Picchu in Peru. It was located high in the Andes Mountains. With a guide, they traveled to the ruins on mules.

Neruda's visit to the magnificent stone fortress proved to be a moment of great importance for him. As he later wrote:

> I felt infinitely small in the center of that navel of rocks, the navel of a deserted world, proud, towering high, to which I somehow belonged. . . . I felt Chilean, Peruvian, American. On those difficult heights, among those glorious, scattered ruins, I had found the principles of faith I needed to continue my poetry.[8]

After the visit, he wrote one of his most famous

**Neruda takes in the view at Machu Picchu, the ruins of a great Incan city in Peru.**

## Machu Picchu

The walled city of Machu Picchu was built by the Incas, Peru's last great Indian civilization. The ruins of the city cling to a steep mountain ridge in the Andes, almost eight thousand feet above sea level. The city's huge stones were shaped and fitted together so perfectly that only gravity was needed to keep them in place. The Incas built the city around 1450. The Spaniards conquered the Incas in the 1530s, but they never found the high mountain fortress. An American explorer discovered Machu Picchu in 1911 and told the world. Today more than five hundred thousand tourists a year visit the stone ruins high in the clouds.

poems, "Alturas de Macchu Picchu" ("The Heights of Macchu Picchu"). (He spelled the first part of the name with an extra "c.") He explained that his visit to the Incan city helped him see the connection between ancient and modern man. "I thought about ancient American man," he wrote. "I saw his ancient struggles intermeshed with present-day struggles. . . . Now I saw the whole of America from the heights of Macchu Picchu."[9]

Neruda and his wife visited Uruguay and Argentina before they returned home to Santiago, Chile, in November 1943. Neruda resumed his active social life in the capital city and also devoted himself to his

## "The Heights of Macchu Picchu"

In these lines from one of his greatest poems, Neruda remembers the lives of the workers who built the magnificent stone city:

Down through the blurred splendor,
down through the night of stone, let me plunge my hand
and let the ancient heart of the forgotten
throb within me
like a bird imprisoned for a thousand years!
Today let me forget this joy which is wider than the sea,
because man is wider than the sea and all her islands,
and one must fall into him as into a well in order to rise
from the depths
with a branch of secret water and sunken truths.[10]

writing. The need to take part in the political life of his country became greater than ever. The government of Chile was a representative democracy with a president elected from an array of political parties.

Neruda had long been in sympathy with the Communists who opposed the fascist forces in Europe. This conflict began with the Spanish Civil War and continued with the Axis powers at war in Europe. In 1944, the Communist Party asked Neruda to be its candidate for senator of the two northern provinces of Chile. These provinces were located in the Atacama desert, home of Chile's mining industry. Miners in the northern provinces had fought for years for better working conditions and higher wages.

Neruda agreed to campaign by reading his poetry to the people. He was shocked at the poverty and bleakness of life in the desert provinces. "There are few places in the world where life is so harsh and offers so little to live for," he wrote. "I had a childhood filled with rain and snow. The mere act of facing that lunar desert was a turning-point in my life."[11] "My heart is still shuddering with the memory of the poverty of those camps."[12]

Neruda was elected senator for the desert provinces in March 1945. (In July, he became an official member of Chile's Communist Party.) "I shall always cherish with pride the fact that thousands of people from Chile's most inhospitable region, the great mining region of copper and nitrate, gave me their vote. . . . My poetry opened the way for communication," he wrote.[13]

In May 1945, Neruda became the first poet to receive Chile's National Prize for Literature. He felt deeply the responsibilities he held as a writer and as an elected member of the government of Chile. His voice was not only one of personal expression but of public opinion, too.

Neruda spent the fall of 1945 working on his poetry at his seaside home, Isla Negra. He learned in November that his friend and fellow poet Gabriela Mistral had become the first Latin American to win the Nobel Prize for Literature. At the beginning of 1946, Neruda received the Order of the Aztec Eagle from the government of Mexico. His reputation as a writer and a statesman continued to grow throughout Latin America and the world. Translations of his work appeared in Europe and the United States.

> **"I had a childhood filled with rain and snow."**

Later that spring, Neruda agreed to serve as campaign organizer for one of Chile's presidential candidates, Gabriel González Videla. The Communists and others backed González Videla. He appeared to be the candidate best suited to represent the party's goals. Neruda traveled throughout Chile speaking for the candidate. González Videla won the election by a narrow margin. He soon began to turn against many who had supported him. In October 1946, he fired all Communist government ministers.

After World War II, an undeclared political and economic war began between former allies, the United States and the Soviet Union. Called the Cold War, the rivalry between the two powers spread around the world. In Chile, the United States had great economic interests, particularly in the mines of the north. González Videla may have turned against his Communist supporters to gain favor with the United States and the anti-Communist forces in Chile. He agreed to a violent attack on striking coal miners and banned the Communist Party in Chile.

At the end of 1947, Pablo Neruda spoke out against the president he had helped to elect. He first wrote an article for a Venezuela newspaper condemning González Videla's actions. Then he spoke out against him in a speech in Chile's Senate. Neruda wrote, "I am proud of any personal risk suffered in this battle for dignity, culture, and freedom—a struggle all the more imperative for being tied to the future of Chile and to the unbounded love I feel for the country I have so often sung in my poetry."[14] González Videla struck back. He revoked Neruda's status as a senator. Without his standing as a senator, Neruda was subject to arrest as a member of the Communist Party. He became a wanted man in his own country, on the run from government forces.

# 7

# Poet-in-Exile

In January 1948, Pablo Neruda went into hiding. An attempt to escape to Argentina failed, and he began a secret life in his native land. For a year, he and Delia moved from one location to another, staying with friends to avoid capture. Across Chile, members of the Communist Party were being arrested and imprisoned. As a well-known political and literary figure, Neruda would be easily recognized if he appeared in public.

The Communist Party assigned a young history student, Alvaro Jara Hantke, the task of keeping Neruda and his wife safe. They were moved from house to house every few weeks, often leaving in the middle of the night. Keeping quiet and out of sight was not Neruda's natural way of life. He loved to walk the streets, shop in the markets, and socialize with his friends at home and out in the world.

Neruda's safety and freedom depended on the help of his friends. For all of 1948, he lived secretly in the

city apartments and country houses of loyal admirers
who put themselves in danger to help him. During his
year in hiding, Neruda continued work on his *Canto
General*. He wrote about the land and the people, past
and present. Jara Hantke described the sound of
Neruda clattering away on his portable typewriter and
noted that his life in hiding at least gave Neruda plenty
of time to work on his poetry.[1] Neruda wrote during the
day, and at night he read his poetry to the friends who
were sheltering him. He refused to give up his beloved
dinner parties and celebrations, even when he was
warned that the noise might reveal his whereabouts.

**Neruda's false identity papers from his year in hiding in Chile named
him Antonio Ruiz Lagoretta.**

In the Chilean winter months of June and July 1948, Neruda and Delia were hidden with friends in the seacoast city of Valparaíso. Neruda had visited Valparaíso as a student. The city, perched on steep hillsides overlooking the Pacific Ocean, fascinated him. At that time, friends hoped to smuggle Neruda out of Chile on a ship. Neruda kept writing and enjoyed watching the busy streets he could see from his window. "Trapped as I was in my corner," he wrote, "my curiosity knew no bounds."[2]

Neruda celebrated his forty-fourth birthday with a party on July 12, 1948. Plans to leave Valparaíso by ship did not work out. Neruda wrote with humor about the new suit that his host family bought him for the trip. "I've never had so much fun as I had when I received it," he wrote. "The women of the house took their notions of style from a celebrated film of the day: *Gone With the Wind*."[3] Neruda never lost his sense of humor or his joy of living even in the riskiest and most uncomfortable situations.

By December 1948, Neruda and Delia were once again hiding in Santiago. Their protector, Jara Hantke, agreed to help them organize a Christmas party for all their friends. Everyone gathered at a secret location. No one could leave the party until Neruda and his wife were safely back in hiding. In the hot months of January and February 1949, Neruda wrote the final verses of his *Canto General*. At last, plans were ready for an attempt to move Neruda out of Chile. An exciting and very dangerous journey was about to begin. Neruda would travel on horseback across the Andes Mountains into Argentina.

Wearing dark glasses and a heavy beard, Neruda began the escape huddled in the backseat of a car. Friends drove him south from Santiago into the forests of southern Chile. On the road, they passed by Neruda's childhood home in Temuco. He later wrote about his feelings as he watched from the car window, "It was my childhood saying goodbye. . . . My poetry was born between the hill and the river, it took its voice from the rain. . . . And now on the road to freedom, I was pausing for a moment near Temuco and could hear the voice of the water that had taught me to sing."[4]

The car headed for a lumber mill in the foothills. From the mill, a group of experienced cowboys would guide Neruda through a rugged mountain pass used by smugglers. Neruda had only a few days to practice his horsemanship. He had not been on a horse since his childhood, and the ride would

> **"My poetry was born between the hill and the river."**

be long and difficult. On March 8, 1949, the group set out. Neruda was carrying a set of false identification papers and a typed copy of *Canto General*. His book was disguised with a false cover and a false title, *Risas y Lagrimas* (*Laughter and Tears*).

The mountain crossing took four days. Twice Neruda's life was in danger, once when his horse

Neruda made his escape from Chile across the Andes Mountains in March 1949.

struggled to cross a raging river. The horse later slipped on jagged rocks and fell. "I was thrown from my horse and left sprawled out on the rocks more than once. My horse was bleeding from the nose and legs, but we stubbornly continued on our vast, magnificent, grueling way," he wrote.[5] The riders had to hack their way through fallen trees and brush before finally reaching the Argentinean side of the mountain pass and freedom.

Once in Argentina, Neruda was driven to the capital city of Buenos Aires. More troubles awaited him. He had escaped the clutches of the police in Chile, but the government of Argentina had been asked to capture him if he managed to cross the border. He had to remain in hiding until he could leave South America. Luckily, Neruda seldom ran short of friends willing to help.

Miguel Angel Asturias, the writer Neruda had met in Guatemala several years before, was now working in Argentina. The two men were good friends. They also looked alike. They had once laughed about their resemblance to turkeys. "Long-nosed, with plenty to spare in the face and body, we shared a resemblance to the succulent bird," Neruda wrote.[6] Asturias offered to let Neruda borrow his passport and his identity in order to leave Argentina and travel to Europe.

Within days, posing as Asturias, Neruda had crossed the River Plate from Argentina to Uruguay and set sail for France. Now that he had escaped the danger in his home country, where would he go? He was famous around the world, not only as a poet, but also as an outspoken member of the Communist Party. Many countries during the Cold War would not welcome a Communist political activist like Neruda.

Once he arrived in France, he became Pablo Neruda again. Now, he needed the help of friends like the artist Pablo Picasso, who appealed to the French government to permit Neruda to remain legally in France. "He spoke to the authorities; he called up a good many people," Neruda wrote of his friend. "I don't know how many marvelous paintings he failed to paint on account of me."[7]

*Neruda celebrated joyfully with old friends and new.*

Picasso was delighted to present Neruda as a surprise visitor to the Congress of Partisans of Peace meeting in Paris on April 25, 1949. After the peace conference, Neruda celebrated joyfully with old friends and new. One friend wrote that Neruda was "the man of the hour in the center of the world, hungrily listening and talking, granting ten interviews a day."[8] While in Paris, Neruda met the writer Ilya Ehrenburg, who would soon begin translating Neruda's poetry into Russian. Neruda's poetry had become an international tool of friendship. In the coming years, while he was still a political fugitive from Chile, his poetry would often make friends for Neruda even among his enemies.

In June 1949, Neruda visited the Soviet Union for the first time. He attended the celebration of the 150th anniversary of the birth of the Russian writer Alexander Pushkin, one of Neruda's many literary heroes. Neruda toured Moscow and Leningrad. He enjoyed visiting the scene of the Russian novels he had read as a boy. In July 1949, his wife Delia was able to rejoin Neruda in Poland for his forty-fifth birthday. From Poland, they traveled to Hungary, Romania, and Czechoslovakia. Translations of Neruda's poetry were beginning to appear in these countries and around the world.

In August 1949, Neruda and Delia left Europe and sailed back across the ocean to Latin America for a peace conference in Mexico City. Neruda was happy to return to Mexico and was greeted warmly by friends in the capital city. Neruda's home once again became a busy center for social gatherings. On Chile's independence day, September 18, Neruda and his wife hosted a celebration. Three hundred guests visited their small apartment, even though Neruda was in bed with a fever.

Neruda's fever was the result of phlebitis, the inflamation of a vein in his leg. He hired a nurse to help out while he was disabled. His nurse, Matilde Urrutia, was a woman from the south of Chile. Neruda had met her three years earlier in Santiago. She was a singer and actress living and working temporarily in Mexico. Neruda and Urrutia formed a close bond that would draw them together in the coming years.

In March 1950, Neruda's *Canto General*, the manuscript of poems he had smuggled over the Andes the previous year, was published in Mexico City.

Mexican artists Diego Rivera and David Alfaro Siqueiros created illustrations for the book. At the same time, an edition of the book was also being published secretly in Chile from a copy of the poems Neruda had left behind. After a brief visit to Guatemala, Neruda and Delia set sail for Europe once again. Neruda was still a fugitive, unable to return to his own country. For two more years, he would travel constantly, seeking a safe and peaceful haven.

In his travels, Neruda attended peace conferences and writers' conferences and gave readings of his poetry. In January 1951, he visited Italy and read his poetry to large, enthusiastic crowds. The Italian government, however, informed him that he was not welcome. He would have to avoid making any political statements while in Italy.

The French government threatened to deny him residence in France. Neruda and Delia traveled instead to Berlin, Germany. There, Neruda met again with Matilde Urrutia, his former nurse, who had come to Europe to perform with a Chilean musical group. Urrutia wrote later that Neruda gave her a hug and said, "I never want to be away from you again."[9] Neruda began writing a series of love poems for her that would become *Los Versos del Capitán* (*The Captain's Verses*).

In September 1951, Neruda took a train journey with Delia and Ilya Ehrenburg east across the vast expanse of the Soviet Union. Then they flew to Mongolia and traveled on to Peking, China. The following month they were back in Europe, visiting Prague, Czechoslovakia, Austria, and Switzerland. Neruda spent the year's end in Italy, visiting Rome, Florence, and Naples, giving readings of his poetry.

In January 1952, the Naples police told Neruda he would have to leave Italy. His permit to stay for three months was cancelled. Neruda and Delia left Naples by train for Rome. As the train pulled in to the station in Rome, they saw a large crowd of people waiting. People were shouting, "Pablo, Pablo" and "Let the poet stay!" as the police tried to keep order. Finally, the police prevented a riot by promising the unruly crowd that Neruda would be allowed to stay in Italy.[10]

Later that month, Neruda accepted an offer to stay in a friend's home on the island of Capri off the west

### Il Postino

In 1995, Pablo Neruda's stay on the island of Capri came to life on the movie screen. An Italian film called *Il Postino* (*The Postman*) features Neruda as a character. A lonely young man from a poor village gets the job of delivering mail to Pablo Neruda. Neruda receives a flood of mail, much of it from women. The young postman decides that being a poet is the way to find love. He asks Neruda to teach him. Neruda and the postman learn from one another about life and love. *Il Postino* shows in a beautiful way the affection that Neruda and his work inspired in ordinary people everywhere.

**After receiving permission to stay in Italy, Pablo Neruda arrived at the island of Capri on January 18, 1952.**

coast of Italy. Neruda asked Delia to return to Chile. His new love, Matilde Urrutia, and her small dog came to stay with him on Capri. Neruda would spend the last few months of his foreign exile in a peaceful and beautiful setting. He complained to Urrutia that the ocean around their island home did not compare to the coast of his beloved Chile: "If only this sea roared! Its tame waters come to the shore almost silently here; besides, it doesn't smell like our sea."[11] Neruda's book of love poems, *Los Versos del Capitán*, was published anonymously in Naples that summer.

In June 1952, Neruda received the good news that he could return home to Chile. Luckily, his friend Gabriela Mistral was serving as Chilean consul in Rome. Mistral helped obtain a visa for Urrutia too and also arranged for her dog to travel home with her to Chile. Together Neruda and Urrutia boarded a ship from France for the voyage to South America.

# Poet at Home

"Neruda, Neruda!" shouted the welcoming crowd in Santiago. After his long absence from Chile, the poet made his first public appearance in his home country on August 12, 1952. He vowed to keep speaking out for social justice. "We have more copper than anywhere else on the planet. But our children do not have shoes," he told the crowd.[1]

The Communist Party was still officially banned in Chile. But the government was no longer arresting its members. In the fall of 1952, Neruda used his popular support to campaign for presidential candidate Salvador Allende. Neruda traveled throughout Chile speaking and reading his poetry. It was his chance to get back in touch with his country. Neruda's personal life was troubled. He was again living with his wife, Delia. He also spent time with Matilde Urrutia. Neruda loved both women. He knew he would soon have to make a heart-breaking decision between them.

Neruda worked hard for Allende's campaign, but Allende was defeated by General Carlos Ibáñez del Campo. Ibáñez kept his campaign promise to lift the ban on the Communist Party. In December 1952, Neruda began a series of yearly trips to the Soviet Union to attend political and literary conferences. In later years, he served on the committee that awarded the Stalin Peace Prize (later the Lenin Peace Prize). Neruda himself was awarded the prize in December of the following year.

Back in Chile in January 1953, Neruda plunged into work for both his public and his writing life. Neruda later wrote that his years in Chile from 1952 to 1957 were quiet, ". . . and nothing out of the ordinary happened to me."[2] In fact, the 1950s were busy, creative years. He organized a conference, the Continental Congress of Culture, to be held in Santiago in May 1953. Writers and artists from all over the world were invited. Neruda spoke to the conference about his goals for equality and social justice for all people. In his speech, he quoted

**Matilde Urrutia wears a wedding ring that Neruda gave her during a secret ceremony in which the two of them were "married by the moon" in Capri, Italy.**

American poet Walt Whitman, one of his literary and political heroes. Neruda explained his feeling that poetry should be available to all. "We know that poetry is like bread, and must be shared by everyone, the literate and the peasants, by all our vast, incredible, extraordinary family of peoples."[3]

During 1953, Neruda used the money from the Lenin Peace Prize to begin building a special house in Santiago. He called it La Chascona, in honor of Matilde Urrutia. The house would be built on a steep hillside close to the city zoo with a view of the Andes Mountains. In June 1954, Neruda decided to donate his large and valuable collection of books and seashells to the University of Chile. He said of the objects he had gathered with love, "Here is a collection of the beauty which dazzled me."[4] On July 12, 1954, Neruda celebrated his fiftieth birthday with a gala party at his home at Isla Negra.

Also in the year 1954, Neruda published his *Odas Elementales* (*Elementary Odes*). This was the first of a series of books of odes, poems of praise. In his odes, Neruda pointed out the wonder of ordinary things. *Odas Elementales* was a huge success with readers and critics. Neruda brought out two more books of odes, *Nuevas Odas Elementales* (*New Elementary Odes*) in 1956 and *Tercer Libro de las Odas* (*Third Book of Odes*) in 1957. According to one critic, Neruda wanted the odes to surprise people with new visions of ordinary objects, "helping us to see . . . the marvelous significance of the world in which we live."[5] Neruda's collections of odes include such poems as "Ode to the Artichoke," "Ode to My Suit," "Ode to Bicycles," and the playful "Ode to Socks."

Early in 1955, Neruda asked Delia del Carril for a divorce. The end of his marriage caused a sad break with many of his old friends. They did not approve of his decision. He wrote little poetry for the rest of that year, but he traveled widely and continued his poetry readings. He visited the Soviet Union, China, Eastern Europe, Brazil, Uruguay, and Argentina before returning to Chile early in 1956.

In February 1956, Neruda and Communists around the world were stunned to learn from the

> **"This revelation . . . left us in a painful state of mind."**

Soviet Union about crimes committed by the regime of Josef Stalin. Neruda wrote, "This revelation, which was staggering, left us in a painful state of mind."[6] Neruda kept his faith in Communism even though he knew about human rights abuses in Communist regimes. He continued to believe that Communism offered the best hope for social justice.

Neruda and Matilde Urrutia spent most of 1957 away from Chile. He began to write *Cien Sonetos de Amor* (*One Hundred Love Sonnets*) for Urrutia that year. Neruda's Communist politics made him unwelcome in many countries during the Cold War era. When he stopped in Argentina to give a series of poetry readings, he was arrested in his hotel on April 11, 1957, and taken to jail. With the help of writers and friends both in Argentina and other countries, Neruda was released a day and a half later. "I was about to leave the prison," Neruda wrote, "when one of the uniformed guards came up to me and put a sheet of paper on my hands. It was a poem he had dedicated to me. . . . I imagine few poets have received a poetic homage from the men assigned to guard them."[7]

Neruda and Urrutia traveled to Asia. They visited Colombo in Ceylon and Rangoon, where Neruda had served as consul from Chile thirty years before. He found the house where he had lived in Colombo. "I had a hard time finding it," he wrote. "The old place where I had written so many painful poems was going to be torn down soon."[8] Neruda also looked for news of his servant, Brampy, and his friend, Josie Bliss. He found out nothing about either of them.

From Rangoon, Neruda and Urrutia flew to China. They took a trip down the Yangtse River. Neruda celebrated his fifty-third birthday in China. From China, they traveled on to Moscow and spent several months visiting the Soviet republics of Abkhazia and Armenia. Neruda enjoyed the wonderful new landscapes and cultures. He called the Armenian capital city of Erevan "one of the most beautiful cities I have seen. Built of volcanic tuff, it has the harmony of a pink rose."[9]

Neruda's gift for humor, wonder, and delight helped him find joy in almost everything he saw. In Erevan, he visited the city zoo:

> I went straight to the condor's cage, but my country-man did not recognize me. There he stood in a corner of his cage, bald-pated, with the skeptical eyes of a condor without illusions. . . . My experience with the tapir was something different. Erevan's zoo is one of the few that own a tapir from the Amazon, the remarkable animal with an ox's body, a long-nosed face, and beady eyes. I must confess that tapirs look like me.[10]

In October 1957, Neruda and Urrutia visited Finland and Sweden before boarding a ship back to Chile. During his long year of worldwide travel, Neruda wrote poetry at an amazing pace. The first collection of his complete works was published that year. Back at Isla Negra as 1958 began, Neruda embarked on another

## Condor

The Andean condor of South America is the world's largest bird of prey. A member of the vulture family, it has black feathers on its body, a bare head and neck, and a wingspan of up to ten feet wide. One flap of its powerful wings each hour can keep the condor soaring and gliding for long distances. Like all vultures, the condor eats the remains of dead animals. Like the California condor, the condor of the Andes is an endangered bird. A symbol of freedom and majesty, the condor is the national bird of Chile.

presidential campaign tour. Once again he traveled the length and breadth of Chile in support of Salvador Allende. Allende did not win the election, but he came much closer than before.

In 1958, Neruda published a new book, *Estravagario*. He invented this name for a collection of poems about himself and his humorous thoughts on life. He saw himself as complex, puzzling, and full of contradictions.

> ## "I'm not always an easy person."

In early 1959, Neruda and Urrutia visited Venezuela. During a stay of several months, Neruda was named an honorary citizen of the capital city of Caracas.

In Caracas, Neruda met Fidel Castro, leader of a revolutionary government that had just seized power in Cuba. Governments in Latin America looked at events in Cuba with great interest. The United States saw Castro's revolution as a threat to political stability in Latin America.

In December 1959, Neruda published his *Cien Sonetos de Amor* written for Urrutia. He told a writer friend how much she helped him in his life and work:

> [Matilde] has patience with my whims and co-operates so that I can live as I want, and write comfortably . . . I'm not always an easy person . . . She organizes my trips. She deals with all the accounts, and this is very good for a poet, isn't it? Good for a husband and even better for a poet.[11]

Urrutia helped the poet both by inspiring him and creating an orderly life at home and on the road.

In Chile, 1960 was a year of political and economic unrest. Workers all over the country protested low wages and lack of opportunity for a better life. In April, Neruda returned to Moscow once again for the Lenin Peace Prize presentation. He also visited Poland, Bulgaria, Romania, and Czechoslovakia before settling in Paris for the autumn of 1960. There he received the terrible news that a huge earthquake had struck southern Chile. Many towns and cities were heavily damaged. The seaside resort of Puerto Saavedra, where Neruda had spent happy childhood vacations, was destroyed by a tsunami, a giant tidal wave caused by the powerful earthquake.

Neruda returned to Chile in November 1960. He found his new home in Valparaíso seriously damaged by the recent earthquake. Neruda had fallen in love with the seaport city of Valparaíso during his year in hiding in 1948. Before leaving on his travels in the spring of 1960, he had bought a home there. He called the house La Sebastiana after a former owner. It was on a hillside with a view of the ocean. Now the house, full of many of Neruda's books and other treasures, had a collapsed floor.

Urrutia wrote that Neruda was especially worried about his big wooden horse from Temuco: "The horse originally came from a hardware store that Pablo passed by every day as he walked to grammar school. He'd always stop to admire it and pet its muzzle. He grew up with the horse and came to consider it somehow his

**The Nerudas moved into a house called La Sebastiana in the town of Valparaíso.**

**Pablo and Matilde Neruda visit their wooden horse, Carousel, in Valparaíso, Chile.**

own."[12] Years later, Neruda had been able to buy the Temuco horse and bring it to Valparaíso. His house, La Sebastiana, was repaired. Neruda and Urrutia held a housewarming there on Chile's national holiday, September 18, 1961.

Books of poetry continued to flow from Pablo Neruda's remarkable imagination. He maintained his schedule of writing every day, most often by hand using his favorite green ink. His work had been translated into languages around the world. Everywhere he traveled, people knew him. In 1961, his Buenos Aires publisher, Losada, printed the one millionth copy of

Neruda's most popular book, *Twenty Love Poems and a Song of Despair*.[13]

That year he received an honorary doctorate degree from Yale University in the United States. The following year he began a series of twelve articles about his life for a magazine in Brazil. He would later use the stories as material for his memoirs. In addition to his poetry, Neruda produced many newspaper and magazine articles. He also gave readings and speeches around Chile and throughout the world. He approached his sixtieth birthday as a world-renowned literary and political figure.

# 9

# Isla Negra

On Neruda's sixtieth birthday, a newspaper reporter asked him if he had achieved his dreams. Neruda said he felt that his life had gone just fine. He said his writing was not exactly a dream but simply something that was part of him. "For me, writing poetry is like seeing and hearing—it's something inherent in me."[1]

A new collection of poems appeared on Neruda's birthday in July 1964, *Memorial de Isla Negra*. The book was named for Neruda's favorite writing place, his seaside home at Isla Negra. It contained poems about his early life—his childhood, his parents, his loves, and his fears. Once again in 1964, Neruda traveled throughout Chile campaigning for Salvador Allende in the presidential election. Allende was defeated yet again.

Early the following year, Neruda and Matilde Urrutia traveled to Europe. In June, Neruda received an honorary doctorate degree from Oxford University in England. He was the first Latin American to receive this honor. From England, they traveled to France for the month of July and then on to Budapest, Hungary. Neruda's summer travels took him to conferences of writers and peace workers. From Hungary, Neruda traveled to Yugoslavia, Finland, and Russia.

In Yugoslavia, Neruda met American playwright Arthur Miller. Miller invited Neruda to come to the United States the following year for the PEN Club writer's conference. Neruda knew the U.S. government would not welcome a Communist poet. Miller promised to help get permission for Neruda's visit. In June 1966, Neruda and Urrutia arrived in New York. Writers from around the world gathered for the thirty-fourth International PEN Congress. Arthur Miller reported that Neruda loved New York and spent many happy hours in the bookshops buying copies of Shakespeare and Walt Whitman.[2] Crowds of fans flocked around Neruda while he was in New York. He also visited Washington, D.C., to record his poems for the Library of Congress. Then he traveled west to California. Neruda stopped in Mexico and Peru to give readings of his poetry before returning to Chile.

On October 28, 1966, Neruda married Matilde Urrutia. Their wedding took place at Isla Negra with friends looking on. The following month, Neruda published a new collection of poems, *Arte de Pájaros* (*The Art of Birds*). The poems were not only about the real birds of Chile, which Neruda knew very well. He also included imaginary birds such as "The Shebird" and "The Mebird" for Matilde and Pablo. Illustrated with pictures, *Arte de Pájaros*, combined Neruda's love of nature and his great sense of fun.

Neruda spent as much time as possible at Isla Negra. The house by the ocean was filled with his treasures relating to the sea and sailing. His book *Una Casa en la Arena (A House in the Sand)*, published in 1966, described the house at Isla Negra. The names of friends who had died were carved on the wooden ceiling beams. A carved figure from the front of an old sailing ship hung from the ceiling. A ship's anchor rested in the sand in front of the house.

Although his health was failing, Neruda kept up his yearly travel to Europe for peace congresses and writers' conferences. In May 1967, he attended the Congress of Soviet Writers in Moscow. Neruda stayed in the home of a Russian friend. The friend wrote, "One of the first people to greet Pablo at the apartment was an old floor-polisher, who carefully wiped his hand before shaking Neruda's and then, to Pablo's delight, began to recite one of Neruda's poems by heart."[3] The poetry of Neruda had circled the globe. It found its way into the hearts of ordinary people everywhere.

From Moscow, Neruda and Matilde visited Italy, France, and England. They attended the International Poetry Conference in London. There, Neruda renewed

> **The poetry of Neruda had circled the globe.**

his friendship with Mexican poet Octavio Paz who later called Neruda, "the greatest poet of his generation. By far!"[4] Neruda returned to Chile in August 1967 and resumed his busy writing and speaking schedule.

His next poetry collection, *La Barcarola* (*The Barcarole*) was published in December. Neruda expanded one of the poems from the collection into a play. It told the story of the legendary bandit Joaquin Murieta. Neruda enjoyed the experience of writing and producing a work for the stage. In Neruda's version of the tale of the 1849 California Gold Rush, Joaquin Murieta is a native of Chile.

Neruda was in his mid-sixties in 1968 and in poor health, but his creative energy still burned strong. The third edition of his complete poems, published in July 1968 by Losada of Buenos Aires, now filled two volumes. Neruda continued to work at both poetry and politics. Politics, for him, was being involved in the life of the world. It was concern for his fellow man. In an interview for a Mexican newspaper, Neruda said, "You cannot be happy if you do not fight for other people's happiness. . . . Man cannot be a happy island."[5]

In September 1969, the Communist Party asked Neruda to put his name in the running for their candidate for President of Chile in the 1970 elections. To his surprise, Neruda won the nomination. The wave of popular support amazed him. "I was in demand everywhere," he wrote. "I was moved by the hundreds and thousands of ordinary men and women who

**Neruda briefly ran for president of Chile in 1970. While campaigning, he visited people in the countryside.**

crushed me to them and kissed me and wept. . . . I spoke or read my poems to them all in pouring rain, in the mud on streets and roads, in the south wind that sends shivers through each of us."[6] In the end, Neruda decided to step down from the presidential race. He gave his support instead to another candidate he believed in, Salvador Allende.

Political and economic unrest continued in Chile through the months leading up to the September 1970 election. In a surprise victory, Salvador Allende received the most votes. The Congress of Chile approved his election as president in October. Allende became the world's first democratically elected Communist head of state.[7] Allende's leadership was in danger from the beginning. Forces opposed to his policies, including the government of the United States, began working against him. To Neruda, the situation in Chile looked much like that just before the tragic Spanish Civil War began.[8]

In January 1971, Neruda made a visit to Easter Island, in the South Pacific, 2,300 miles off the coast of Chile. Neruda visited the mysterious volcanic island as host of a television program on the history and geography of Chile. He would publish a book about his visit in 1972, *La Rosa Separada* (*The Separate Rose*).

> **Doctors told Matilde that Neruda had cancer.**

While on Easter Island, Neruda learned that he had a new job. He would become Chile's ambassador to Paris. Neruda had asked for the appointment. President Allende agreed that Neruda would be an excellent representative of Chile in the important European capital. Neruda and Matilde set off for Paris in March 1971. One of Neruda's missions was to meet with bankers about Chile's debt to foreign nations. He also planned to seek personal medical advice from doctors in France.

Soon after he arrived in Paris, Neruda underwent surgery. Doctors told Matilde that Neruda had cancer. She decided it was best not to tell him. Neruda celebrated his sixty-seventh birthday in Paris. He quietly recovered from his operation. Did he know his illness was serious?

## Easter Island

Easter Island is famous for its mysterious stone statues carved hundreds of years ago. More than six hundred huge statues are scattered around the island. Most of the statues are between eleven and twenty feet high. Some rise as high as forty feet. The early people of the island carved the statues from the rock of an extinct volcano. Scientists are still studying the statues. No one knows yet how the giant figures were moved and set up around the island. Today, Polynesian and Chilean people live on Easter Island. It has been governed by Chile since 1888.

These mysterious statues are on Easter Island.

**The king of Sweden presents Pablo Neruda (right) with the Nobel Prize for Literature in December 1971.**

He gave no sign but continued to work steadily. He planned for the future with hope and good humor. In the autumn of 1971, he visited the province of Normandy on the north coast of France. He bought a country house to use as a weekend home. He later wrote that he wanted a house "where we could breathe with the leaves, the water, the birds, the air."[9]

On October 21, 1971, Pablo Neruda received the Nobel Prize for Literature. He and Matilde traveled to Stockholm, Sweden, in December for the awards ceremony. His wife later wrote about Neruda's conversation with the king of Sweden. Neruda and the king shared a love of rocks. Neruda described the enormous rocks of Easter Island and invited the king to visit.[10]

Neruda titled his Nobel Prize acceptance speech "Poetry Shall Not Have Sung In Vain." Neruda always referred to poetry as "song" and to writing poetry as "singing." He began his speech with the story of his exciting escape over the Andes into Argentina in 1949. Then he spoke about poetry and its meaning and usefulness in human life.

"I have often maintained that the best poet is he who prepares our daily bread. . . . He performs his majestic and humble task of kneading the dough, consigning it to the oven, baking it in golden colors and handing us our daily bread as a duty of fellowship," said Neruda.[11] He spoke of his dream of a new "City of Man" ruled by freedom and justice. In the face of his own illness and political unrest in his country, Pablo Neruda never lost hope for the future of mankind.

Pablo Neruda is admired today for his great contributions to the world of literature.

# 10

# A Legacy of Joy

In April 1972, Neruda made his second visit to New York City. He had been invited to speak at the fiftieth anniversary dinner of the United States PEN Club. Neruda told the audience that he owed an enormous debt to his American poetic hero, Walt Whitman:

> As for myself, now a man of almost seventy, I was barely fifteen when I discovered Walt Whitman . . . the poet who measured the earth with long, slow strides, pausing everywhere to love and to examine, to learn, to teach, and to admire. . . . He is the first absolute poet, and it was his intention not only to sing but to impart his vast vision of the relationships of men and of nations.[1]

Neruda always kept a picture of the bearded American poet on his desk. When a workman at Isla Negra asked him if the man in the picture was his grandfather, Neruda replied, "Yes."[2]

During his visit to New York, Neruda once again

visited the shops that sold antiques, seashells, and books. Crowds of admirers flocked around him at all times. He gave poetry readings at the United Nations, the Poetry Center, and Columbia University before returning to Paris. An interviewer asked him how people reacted to his poetry readings. He said, "They love me in a very emotional way. I can't enter or leave some places. . . . That happens everywhere."[3]

Neruda always enjoyed his birthday parties. He celebrated his sixty-eighth birthday at his country home in Normandy, France. He had named the house *La Manquel*, which means "the condor." For his party, he dressed up in costume as he loved to do. He wore a top hat, a red jacket, and a false moustache. His friends often described Neruda as *un gran nino* (a big child), referring to his playful love of life.[4]

One friend who had sheltered Neruda during his year of hiding in Chile gave thanks for the chance to have lived with the poet. "We are grateful to him . . . for teaching us to value the smallest things: the trees in the park, the stones in the sea, old books, textures, smells, tastes. . . . He had an inexhaustible sense of humor."[5] Neruda's joy in being alive showed in his politics and his poetry.

After a second surgery in Paris in October 1972, Neruda decided it was time to return to Chile. He wanted to go home. After resigning his diplomatic post, he left Paris for the last time in November. Although it would soon be summer in Chile, the political climate was not warm or welcoming.

Economic problems plagued the country. Foreign pressures threatened Allende's government. The United States secretly supported plans to overthrow the Allende regime. U.S. President Richard Nixon and his advisers feared the effects of Allende's socialist policies. Allende took ownership of Chile's copper and nitrate industries away from U.S. companies. Nixon cut off trade between the United States and Chile.

Plans were made for a national celebration of Neruda's seventieth birthday in July of the following year. Neruda decided to offer his own birthday gift to the people of Chile. He hoped to complete eight new books in time for the 1974 anniversary. Seven would be new collections of poems, one for each decade of his life. The eighth book would be his memoirs.

> **Neruda decided to offer his own birthday gift to the people of Chile.**

On July 12, 1973, Neruda spent his sixty-ninth birthday quietly with a few friends. He was very weak and remained in bed. One of his visitors was the son of Neruda's publisher. Neruda gave him his seven new book manuscripts. He asked that they be published the following year for his seventieth birthday. He would continue to work on his memoirs for the next two months.

Chilean-American writer Isabel Allende, niece of President Salvador Allende, visited Neruda at Isla Negra that winter. Isabel Allende wrote of her visit, "The poet was not well . . . He was weak, but he found the strength to lead me through the marvelous twists and turns of that cave crammed with his trove of modest treasures and to show me his collections of seashells, bottles, dolls, books and paintings."[6]

Neruda continued to write. He watched the news on television with increasing sorrow. On September 11, 1973, the military forces of Chile, led by General Augusto Pinochet, overthrew the elected government. The presidential palace was bombed. President Allende died in the fight that followed. Thousands of Chilean civilians were also killed. Neruda wrote the final lines of his memoirs shortly after that day.

Neruda's health declined quickly. Matilde transported him from Isla Negra to a medical clinic in Santiago. He died there on Sunday, September 23, 1973, with his wife and his sister, Laura, by his side. Matilde decided to have a memorial service for Neruda at La Chascona, their house in Santiago. The house had been ransacked by the military police and was badly damaged. Neruda's wife thought it might help the people of Chile for foreign journalists and diplomats to come to the house and see what the military forces had done. They had even destroyed the home of a beloved national poet.

On September 25, Neruda's casket was carried through the streets of Santiago to the General

**Pablo Neruda is buried next to Matilde Urrutia behind his house, Isla Negra.**

Cemetery. The people of the city were forbidden to assemble in large groups. Many risked the danger to follow Neruda's funeral procession. The crowd began to sing and cheer. Armed soldiers watched them with guns ready.

Although his final days were filled with sorrow for his country, Neruda's legacy of joy and hope lives on. His vast outpouring of poetry, more than thirty-five hundred pages, has been translated into more than thirty languages around the world. Because Neruda's poetry is available to most of the world's population, one translator calls him "probably the most-read poet in human history."[7] Another translator thanks Neruda "for his generous legacy of beauty and love, his reverence for life, his plea for justice and equality, peace and goodwill."[8]

Colombian writer Gabriel García Márquez called Neruda "the greatest poet of the twentieth century—in any language."[9] Each season of Neruda's life gave him a new direction for his poetry and something new to discover and enjoy. He once told an interviewer, "For me writing is like breathing. I could not live without breathing and I could not live without writing."[10] Neruda's passionate connection to life made the words he wrote "closer to blood than to ink." Readers feel his connection to their lives. His poems ring true in their hearts and stay in their memories.

## Pablo Neruda Foundation

After Neruda's death, his wife Matilde took on a special mission. She wanted to preserve his memory by promoting knowledge of the poet and his work. Before her death in 1985, she made plans for the Pablo Neruda Foundation. The foundation restored Neruda's three houses and established a library for scholars. Today the foundation manages the literary legacy of Pablo Neruda. It grants permission to publish his work and uses money earned to support research and writing projects. The foundation gives awards to promising writers. Each year, it honors the best student at the poet's childhood school in Temuco.

After the military coup of 1973, it took almost twenty years for democracy to return to Chile. In 1992, Pablo Neruda and Matilde Urrutia, who died in 1985, were buried together in front of the house at Isla Negra. Today in Chile, the three homes of Pablo Neruda are cultural centers visited by thousands each year. The Pablo Neruda Foundation at the University of Chile promotes the study and appreciation of his work. Around the world, Neruda continues to inspire new generations of readers and scholars who find his voice and his message irresistibly beautiful. In these final lines from the poem "El Fugitivo: XII," Pablo Neruda expresses his bond of gratitude and love with his readers and with life itself:

> *To all and everyone,*
> *to all I don't know, who'll never*
> *hear this name, to those who live*
> *along our long rivers,*
> *at the foot of volcanoes, in the sulphuric*
> *copper shadow, to fishermen and peasants,*
> *to blue Indians on the shore*
> *of lakes sparkling like glass,*
> *to the shoemaker who at this moment questions,*
> *nailing leather with ancient hands,*
> *to you, to whomever without knowing it has waited for me,*
> *I belong and recognize and sing.[11]*

# Selected Works by Pablo Neruda

*Residence on Earth* (1962)

*The Heights of Macchu Picchu* (1966)

*Twenty Poems* (1967)

*Pablo Neruda: The Early Poems* (1969)

*A New Decade: Poems, 1958–1967* (1969)

*Twenty Love Poems and a Song of Despair* (1969)

*Selected Poems* (1970)

*Stones of the Sky* (1970)

*Neruda and Vallejo: Selected Poems* (1971)

*Extravagaria* (1972)

*New Poems, 1968–1970* (1972)

*Splendor and Death of Joaquin Murieta* (1972)

*The Captain's Verses* (1972)

*Five Decades: A Selection (Poems 1925–1970)* (1974)

*Fully Empowered: Plenos Poderes* (1975)

*Memoirs* (1976)

*Pablo Neruda and Nicanor Parra Face to Face* (1977)

*Isla Negra: A Notebook* (1980)

*Passions and Impressions* (1982)

*Windows That Open Inward: Images of Chile* (1984)

*A Separate Rose* (1985)

*Winter Garden* (1986)

*One Hundred Love Sonnets* (1986)

*The House at Isla Negra* (1988)

*The Sea and the Bells* (1988)

*The Stones of Chile* (1987)

*Late and Posthumous Poems, 1968–1974* (1989)

*Selected Odes of Pablo Neruda* (1990)

*The Yellow Heart* (1990)

*The Book of Questions* (1991)

*Spain in the Heart: Hymn to the Glories of the People at War* (1993)

*Pablo Neruda: An Anthology of Odes* (1994)

*Full Woman, Fleshly Apple, Hot Moon: Selected Poems of Pablo Neruda* (1998)

*The Essential Neruda* (2004)

# Chronology

**1904**—Ricardo Eliecer Neftalí Reyes Basoalto (Pablo Neruda) is born on July 12 in Parral, Chile. His mother dies of tuberculosis one month later.

**1906**—His father remarries and moves the family to Temuco.

**1910**—Neftalí enters Temuco's school for boys.

**1919**—Thirteen of his poems appear in the Santiago magazine *Corre-Vuelva*.

**1920**—Takes the name Pablo Neruda; meets Gabriela Mistral who comes to Temuco as high school principal.

**1921**—Moves to Santiago to study French at the Instituto Pedagogico.

**1924**—*Veinte Poemas de Amor y una Canción Desesperada* is published.

**1927**—Receives appointment as Chilean consul in Rangoon, Burma, and leaves for Asia via Spain and France.

**1928**—Is made Chilean consul in Colombo, Ceylon, and visits India, China, and Japan.

**1930**—Is made Chilean consul in Batavia, Java, and marries Maria Antonieta Hagenaar Vogelzanz.

**1932**—Returns to Santiago, where there is a severe economic depression.

**1933**—Appointed Chilean consul in Buenos Aires, Argentina. Limited edition of *Residencia en la Tierra* is published; meets Federico García Lorca, beginning a deep friendship.

**1934**—Appointed consul in Barcelona, Spain. His daughter, Malva Marina, is born.

**1936**—Spanish Civil War begins. Federico García Lorca is killed by right-wing forces; Neruda loses his consular post.

**1937**—Organizes International Writers Congress in Madrid; *España en el Corazón* is published; returns to Chile.

**1939**—As Chilean consul in charge of emigration of Spanish refugees, Neruda arranges for safe transportation of two thousand refugees to Chile on the *Winnipeg*.

**1940**—Appointed Chilean general consul in Mexico.

**1943**—Divorces from Maria Hagenaar; marries Argentine painter Delia del Carril; resigns his post in Mexico and returns to Chile, stopping first in Peru to visit Machu Picchu.

**1945**—Elected to the senate of Chile and officially joins the Communist Party.

**1947**—Defies Chilean President González Videla and denounces him in an open letter.

**1948**—Is declared an enemy of the government and goes into hiding for a year in Chile.

**1949**—Escapes over the Andes Mountains to Argentina; travels throughout Europe and visits the Soviet Union.

**1950**—*Canto General* is published in Mexico.

**1952**—A new government in Chile revokes Neruda's arrest order; returns to Chile.

**1954**—Divorces Delia del Carril and moves into a new house in Santiago with Matilde Urrutia.

**1964**—*Memorial de Isla Negra* is published.

**1966**—Visits the United States as a guest of the PEN Club in New York; marries Matilde Urrutia on October 28.

**1970**—Runs for president of Chile but steps aside when Salvador Allende enters the race; after Allende's victory, Neruda is appointed ambassador to France.

**1971**—Awarded the Nobel Prize for Literature.

**1972**—Returns to Chile and retires to Isla Negra.

**1973**—Allende's government is overthrown by the military and Allende dies in the attack on September 11; Pablo Neruda dies in a hospital in Santiago on September 23, 1973.

# Chapter Notes

## CHAPTER 1. "HE IS PABLO NERUDA"

1. Volodia Teitelboim, *Neruda: An Intimate Biography* (Austin, Tex.: University of Texas Press, 1991), p. 310.
2. Adam Feinstein, *Pablo Neruda: A Passion for Life* (New York: Bloomsbury, 2004), p. 237.
3. Ibid., p. 309.
4. Ibid., p. 310.
5. Pablo Neruda, *Memoirs* (New York: Farrar, Straus and Giroux, 1974), p. 140.
6. Teitelboim, p. 311.
7. Manuel Duran and Margery Safir, *Earth Tones: The Poetry of Pablo Neruda* (Bloomington, Ind.: Indiana University Press, 1986), p. xiii.

## CHAPTER 2. CHILD OF THE RAIN FOREST

1. Adam Feinstein, *Pablo Neruda: A Passion for Life* (New York: Bloomsbury, 2004), p. 3.
2. Pablo Neruda, *Memoirs* (New York: Farrar, Straus and Giroux, 1974), p. 10.
3. Ibid., p. 6.
4. Feinstein, p. 13.
5. Ibid., p. 12.
6. Volodia Teitelboim, *Neruda: An Intimate Biography* (Austin, Tex.: University of Texas Press, 1991), p.20.
7. Ibid., p. 26.
8. Ibid., p. 22.

9. Neruda, p. 12.

10. Feinstein, p. 10.

11. Pablo Neruda, *Passions and Impressions* (New York: Farrar, Straus and Giroux, 1983), p. 242.

12. Teitelboim, p. 28.

13. Neruda, *Memoirs*, p. 16.

14. Ibid., p. 18.

15. Neruda, *Passions and Impressions*, p. 242.

16. Ibid., p. 241.

17. Neruda, *Memoirs*, p. 21.

18. Ibid.

19. Neruda, *Memoirs*, p. 20.

20. Ibid., p. 16.

21. Ibid., pp. 11–12.

22. Feinstein, p. 22.

23. Neruda, Memoirs, p. 158.

24. Pablo Neruda, "Poetry," *Memorial de Isla Negra*, translated by Alastair Reid, *The Essential Neruda: Selected Poems*, edited by Mark Eisner (San Francisco: City Lights Books, 2004), pp. 167–168.

## CHAPTER 3. SANTIAGO STUDENT POET

1. Pablo Neruda, *Memoirs* (New York: Farrar, Straus and Giroux, 1974), p. 29.

2. Ibid., p. 30.

3. Ibid., p. 32.

4. Ibid.

5. Adam Feinstein, *Pablo Neruda: A Passion for Life* (New York: Bloomsbury, 2004), p. 24.

6. Ibid., p. 30.

7. Neruda, p. 49.

8. Ibid., p. 30.

9. Feinstein, p. 40.

10. Ibid., p. 41.

11. Ibid., p. 43.

12. Ibid., p. 45.

13. Neruda, p. 55.

14. Ibid., p. 64.

15. Ibid., p. 66.

## CHAPTER 4. DIPLOMAT EAST AND WEST

1. Adam Feinstein, *Pablo Neruda: A Passion for Life* (New York: Bloomsbury, 2004), p. 54.

2. Pablo Neruda, *Memoirs* (New York: Farrar, Straus and Giroux, 1974), p. 74.

3. Ibid., p. 86.

4. Ibid.

5. Feinstein, p. 61.

6. Ibid., p. 65.

7. Ibid., p. 64.

8. Ibid., p. 66.

9. Neruda, p. 89.

10. Ibid., p. 102.

11. Ibid., p. 109.

12. Ibid.

13. Feinstein, p. 78.

14. Ibid., p. 80.

15. Ibid., p. 92.

16. Ibid., p. 99.

## CHAPTER 5. CLOSER TO BLOOD THAN TO INK

1. Pablo Neruda, *Memoirs* (New York: Farrar, Straus and Giroux, 1974), p. 116.
2. Ibid.
3. Adam Feinstein, *Pablo Neruda: A Passion for Life* (New York: Bloomsbury, 2004), p. 107.
4. Neruda, p. 124.
5. Volodia Teitelboim, *Neruda: An Intimate Biography* (Austin, Tex.: University of Texas Press, 1991), p. 179.
6. Feinstein, p. 108.
7. Neruda, p. 122.
8. Feinstein, p. 135.
9. Neruda, p. 126.
10. Feinstein, p. 122.
11. Neruda, p. 130.
12. Ibid., p. 133.
13. Feinstein, p. 132.
14. Neruda, p. 147.
15. Pablo Neruda, "The Great Tablecloth," *Estravagario*, translated by Alastair Reid, *The Essential Neruda: Selected Poems*, edited by Mark Eisner (San Francisco: City Lights Books, 2004), p. 139.

## CHAPTER 6. ALL THE AMERICAS

1. Adam Feinstein, *Pablo Neruda: A Passion for Life* (New York: Bloomsbury, 2004), p. 152.
2. Ibid.
3. Pablo Neruda, *Memoirs* (New York: Farrar, Straus and Giroux, 1974), p. 150.
4. Poli Délano, *When I Was a Boy Neruda Called Me Policarpo* (Toronto: Groundwood Books, 2003), pp. 24–25.

5. Feinstein, p. 163.

6. Ibid., p. 167.

7. Neruda, p. 149.

8. Ibid., pp. 165–166.

9. Feinstein, p. 174.

10. Pablo Neruda, "Heights of Macchu Picchu: XI," *Canto general*, translated by Mark Eisner, *The Essential Neruda: Selected Poems*, edited by Mark Eisner (San Francisco: City Lights Books, 2004), p. 89.

11. Neruda, p. 167.

12. Feinstein, p. 180.

13. Neruda, p. 166.

14. Pablo Neruda, *Passions and Impressions* (New York: Farrar, Straus and Giroux, 1978), p. 282.

## CHAPTER 7. POET-IN-EXILE

1. Adam Feinstein, *Pablo Neruda: A Passion for Life* (New York: Bloomsbury, 2004), p. 205.

2. Pablo Neruda, *Memoirs* (New York: Farrar, Straus and Giroux, 1974), p. 174.

3. Ibid., p. 175.

4. Ibid., p. 177.

5. Ibid., p. 183.

6. Ibid., p. 186.

7. Ibid., p. 187.

8. Volodia Teitelboim, *Neruda: An Intimate Biography* (Austin, Tex.: University of Texas Press, 1991), p. 312.

9. Matilde Urrutia, *My Life With Pablo Neruda* (Stanford, Calif.: Stanford General Books, 2004), p. 46.

10. Feinstein, p. 271.

11. Urrutia, p. 104.

## CHAPTER 8. POET AT HOME

1. Adam Feinstein, *Pablo Neruda: A Passion for Life* (New York: Bloomsbury, 2004), p. 184.
2. Pablo Neruda, *Memoirs* (New York: Farrar, Straus and Giroux, 1974), p. 224.
3. Feinstein, p. 292.
4. Ibid., p. 295.
5. Rene de Costa, *The Poetry of Pablo Neruda* (Cambridge: Harvard University Press, 1979), p. 159.
6. Neruda, p. 319.
7. Ibid., p. 225.
8. Ibid., p. 229.
9. Ibid., p. 243.
10. Ibid.
11. Feinstein, p. 322.
12. Matilde Urrutia, *My Life With Pablo Neruda* (Stanford, Calif.: Stanford General Books, 2004), p. 241.
13. Feinstein, p. 330.

## CHAPTER 9. ISLA NEGRA

1. Adam Feinstein, *Pablo Neruda: A Passion for Life* (New York: Bloomsbury, 2004), p. 337.
2. Ibid., p. 343.
3. Ibid., p. 350.
4. Ibid., p. 353.
5. Ibid., p. 365.
6. Pablo Neruda, *Memoirs* (New York: Farrar, Straus and Giroux, 1974), p. 337.
7. Feinstein, p. 373.
8. Ibid., p. 374.
9. Neruda, p. 339.
10. Matilde Urrutia, *My Life With Pablo Neruda* (Stanford, Calif.: Stanford General Books, 2004), p. 278.

11. Pablo Neruda, *Passions and Impressions* (New York: Farrar, Straus and Giroux, 1978), p. 386.

## CHAPTER 10. A LEGACY OF JOY

1. Pablo Neruda, *Passions and Impressions* (New York: Farrar, Straus and Giroux, 1978), pp. 376–377.
2. Adam Feinstein, *Pablo Neruda: A Passion for Life* (New York: Bloomsbury, 2004), p. 386.
3. Rita Guibert, "Pablo Neruda," *Latin American Writers at Work: The Paris Review* (New York: Modern Library, 2003), p. 53.
4. Feinstein, p. 319.
5. Ibid., pp. 213–214.
6. Ibid., p. 404.
7. Alastair Reid, "Introduction," *Pablo Neruda: Selected Poems* (Boston: Houghton Mifflin, 1970).
8. Jack Schmitt, "Translator's Introduction," *Pablo Neruda: Art of Birds* (Austin, Tex.: University of Texas Press, 1985), p. 12.
9. Edward Hirsch, "Pablo Neruda at 100," July 11, 2004, <http://www.washingtonpost.com/wp-dyn/articles/A37885-2004Jul8.html> (June 8, 2006).
10. Guibert, p. 52.
11. Pablo Neruda, "El Fugitivo: XII," *Canto general*, translated by Jack Hirschman, *The Essential Neruda: Selected Poems*, edited by Mark Eisner (San Francisco: City Lights Books, 2004), p. 101.

# Further Reading

Délano, Poli, translated by Sean Higgins. *When I Was a Boy Neruda Called Me Policarpo*. Toronto: Groundwood Books, 2006.

Janeczko, Paul B., ed. *Blushing: Expressions of Love in Poems and Letters*. New York: Orchard Books, 2004.

Kennedy, Caroline, ed. *A Family of Poems: My Favorite Poetry for Children*. New York: Hyperion / Hyperion Books for Children, 2005.

Martinez, Renee Russo, and Leong Wang Shan, ed. *Chile*. Milwaukee, Wis.: Gareth Stevens Pub., 2003.

Ray, Deborah Kogan. *To Go Singing Through the World: The Childhood of Pablo Neruda*. New York: Farrar, Straus and Giroux, 2006.

Salas, Laura Purdie. *Write Your Own Poetry*. Minneapolis, Minn.: Compass Point Books, 2008.

# Internet Addresses

The Pablo Neruda Foundation
   <http://www.fundacionneruda.org/ing/home_ingles.htm>

Pablo Neruda: The Nobel Prize for Literature
   <http://nobelprize.org/nobel_prizes/literature/laureates/
   1971/neruda-bio.html>

Poets.Org from the Academy of American Poets: Pablo
Neruda
   <http://www.poets.org/poet.php/prmPID/279>

# Index